PHOTOSHOP ELEMENTS

NICK VANDOME

in easy steps

LONDON • NEW YORK • SYDNEY • JOHANNESBURG • SINGAPORE • TORONTO • NEW DELHI

In easy steps is an imprint of Computer Step
Southfield Road . Southam
Warwickshire CV47 0FB . England

http://www.ineasysteps.com

Notice of Liability
Every effort has been made to ensure that this book contains accurate and current information. However, Computer Step and the author shall not be liable for any loss or damage suffered by readers as a result of any information contained herein.

Trademarks
Photoshop® is a registered trademark of Adobe Systems Incorporated. All other trademarks are acknowledged as belonging to their respective companies.

Printed and bound in the United Kingdom

ISBN 1-84078-250-1

Contents

Printing images 11 157

Real-world digital examples 12 167

Index 187

Introducing Photoshop Elements

Photoshop Elements is an image editing program that spans the gap between very basic programs and professional-level ones. It is based on the full version of Photoshop but designed with the general user in mind. It can be used to manipulate and enhance digital images and also add special effects, shapes and text. It also offers various options for displaying images on the Web.

This chapter looks at the components of the program and describes their functions.

Covers

Chapter One

Digital imaging overview

Digital photography and image editing have rapidly become transformed from an expensive hobby for the few to a mass market business that is readily available to anyone. The standard and range of digital cameras have improved dramatically in recent years and with the emergence of software such as Photoshop Elements the exciting world of digital imaging is now within everyone's reach. When dealing with digital images there is a reasonable amount of terminology to consider.

Pixels

Images with a higher number of pixels produce larger file sizes.

These are tiny coloured dots that are the building blocks of digital images. The word comes from a contraction of 'picture element' and every image captured with a digital camera or a scanner will contain thousands of pixels. The more pixels there are in an image then, generally, the better as far as the quality is concerned. This is particularly true if the image is going to be printed. The size of an image is usually described in terms of its height and width in pixels, or as these dimensions multiplied together.

Resolution

This is a term that is used to describe a number of things in the world of digital imaging:

- Image resolution. This is the physical size of an image, measured in pixels

- Monitor resolution. This is the number of pixels that can be displayed in a linear inch on a computer monitor (usually 72–96 pixels per inch)

The print resolution of an image is also known as the document size, which refers to the size at which it will be printed.

- Print resolution. This affects the size at which an image can be printed. The print resolution can be altered in the image editing software to alter the print size. A higher print resolution gives a better quality but a smaller image than one with a lower resolution

Image editing software

These are the programs that enhance and improve the basic image from a digital camera or a scanner. The world of image editing is an exciting and versatile one and Photoshop Elements is setting new standards in this field.

Through the use of a program such as Elements, digital images can be improved and altered dramatically:

Original

Improve colour
and composition

Special effects can be added to a whole image, or they can be added to an area that has been selected within an image. For more information on selecting areas, see Chapter Six.

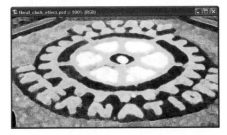

Add special effects

Add items such as
shapes and text

About Elements

Photoshop Elements is the offspring of the professional-level image editing program, Photoshop. Now in its seventh version, Photoshop is somewhat unusual in the world of computer software in that it is widely accepted as being the best program of its type around and there is very little argument about this. If professional designers or photographers are using an image editing program it will almost certainly be Photoshop. However, two of the potential drawbacks to Photoshop are the cost (approximately £525) and its complexity. This is where Elements comes into its own. Adobe (the makers of Photoshop and Elements) have recognised that the majority of digital imaging users (i.e. the consumer market) want something with the basic power of Photoshop but with enough user-friendly features to make it easy to use. With the explosion in the digital camera market a product was needed to meet the needs of a new generation of image editors and that product is Elements.

As well as containing all the important editing/colour management functions that have made Photoshop an undisputed market leader, Elements also combines enough help and guidance features to make the learning curve for new users as smooth as possible:

Photoshop Elements costs approximately £70 and can be bought online from sites like Amazon (www.amazon.com) and Jungle (www.jungle.com) or at computer software retailers. It is also bundled with a lot of digital cameras/scanners.

Elements contains help features such as the Hints palette and the How To palette, which explain what different items can be used for and give a step-by-step guide to various digital techniques

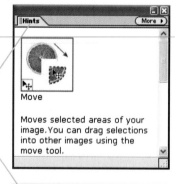

Special effects

One of the great things about using Elements with digital images is that it provides numerous fun and creative options for turning mediocre images into eye-catching works of art. This is achieved through a wide variety of filters and effects:

Effects such as collages can also be created manually. See Chapter Twelve for more details.

Advanced features

In addition to user-friendly features, Elements also has more advanced functions such as the histogram:

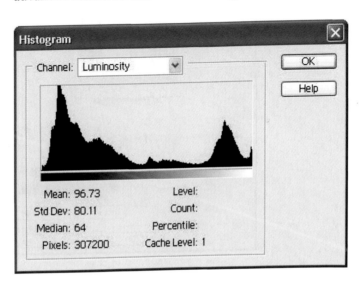

Calibrating your monitor

One of the issues with digital images is achieving consistency between different computer monitors and also output devices, such as printers. This means that the colours can appear different if they are viewed on several monitors and also that the colours in the printed image may not match those viewed on screen. One way to try to achieve as much consistency as possible is to calibrate your monitor before you start working with digital images. This is particularly important if you are going to be sharing images with other people for editing purposes, in which case they should calibrate their monitors too. This will ensure that images look as similar as possible on different machines and so editing can be applied consistently.

A calibrated monitor helps ensure that a printed image is as close as possible to the one you see on your monitor. However, there are also individual printer settings that can influence the final printed image.

To calibrate your monitor (Windows):

1 Make sure your monitor and computer have been turned on for at least 30 minutes

2 Set the monitor display to a minimum of 16-bit colour (or thousands of colours) and set the background colour as neutral

If possible, it is better to set your monitor to display 32-bit colour, which is also known as True Colour.

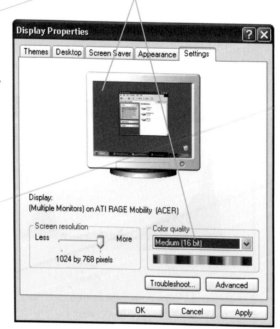

3 Click the Start button and select Control Panel

4 Double-click the Adobe Gamma button

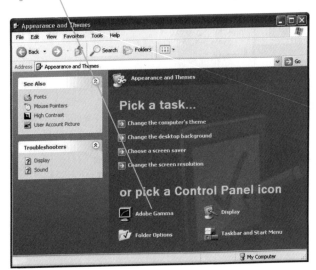

To calibrate a monitor on Mac OS X, open the Finder and select Applications> Utilities>Display Calibrator and follow the wizard's steps.

5 Check on the Step By Step (Wizard) box and click Next to follow the wizard's steps

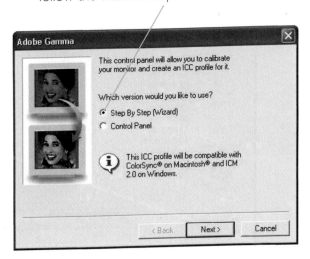

6 Click Finish at the end of the wizard

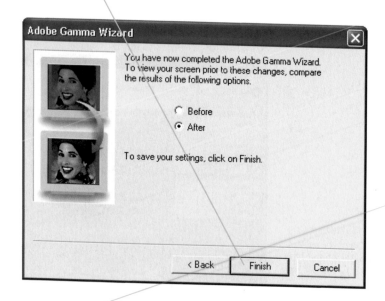

7 Save the colour profile that you have just created

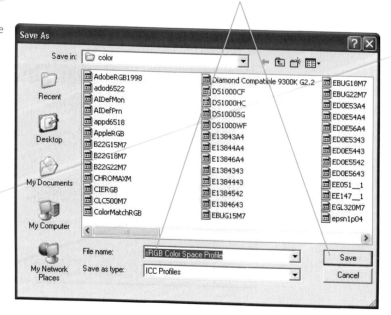

Welcome Screen

When you first open Elements you will be presented with the Welcome Screen. This offers initial advice about working with Elements and also provides options for creating new files or opening existing ones. There is also an option for disabling the Welcome Screen, so that it does not appear every time you open the program. When you become more familiar with Elements, you will probably want to select this option.

Welcome Screen functions

Click here to open a new, blank file

Click here to browse your hard drive for an existing file

Click here to download images from a digital camera or a scanner

The Welcome Screen can be accessed at any time by selecting Window> Welcome from the Menu bar.

Check off this box to disable the Welcome Screen when Elements is opened

Click here for help information

Click here to exit the Welcome Screen

The first view

Once the Welcome Screen has been exited, the standard Elements interface is available. This is a combination of the work area (where images are opened and edited), menus, toolbars, a toolbox and palettes. At first it can seem a little daunting, but Elements has been designed to offer as much help as possible as you proceed through the digital editing process. The interfaces for the Windows and the Mac versions of Elements are almost identical, with the only real difference being the Apple menu and the Photoshop Elements menu on the Mac.

The components of the Elements interface are:

The Mac version of Elements was designed for use on its OS X operating system.

Windows

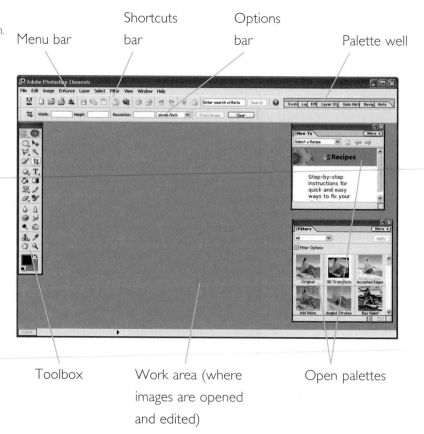

Menu bar

Shortcuts bar

Options bar

Palette well

Toolbox

Work area (where images are opened and edited)

Open palettes

Mac (OS X)

Menu bar Shortcuts bar Options bar Palette well

Toolbox

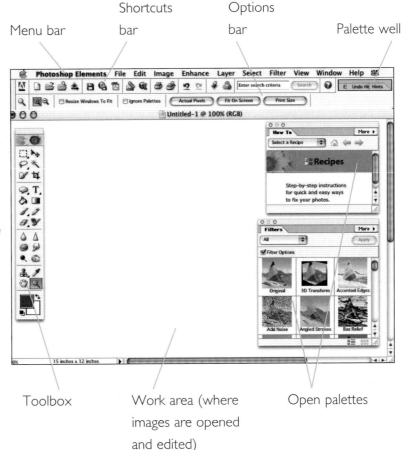

The Windows and the Mac versions of Photoshop Elements are virtually indistinguishable as far as functions and commands are concerned. Any differences will be noted throughout the book where they occur.

Work area (where images are opened and edited)

Open palettes

The Photoshop Elements menu on the Menu bar is one of the very few differences between the Windows version and the Mac version. The most important item on this menu is Preferences

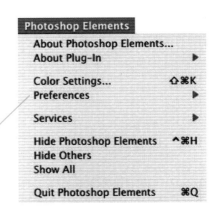

Menu bar

The Menu bar contains menus that provide all of the functionality for the workings of Elements. Some of these functions can also be achieved through the use of the other components of Elements, such as the Toolbox, the Shortcuts bar, the Options bar and the palettes. However, the Menu bar is where all of the commands needed for the digital editing process can be accessed in one place.

Menu bar menus

Elements does not support the CMYK colour model for editing digital images. This could be an issue if you use a commercial printer.

- File. This has standard commands for opening, saving and printing images, and also commands for creating panoramas (Photomerge) and accessing online services from Adobe

- Edit. This contains commands for undoing previous operations and standard copy and paste techniques

- Image. This contains commands for altering the size, shape and position of an image. It also contains more advanced functions such as the colour mode of an image

- Enhance. This contains commands for editing the colour elements of an image. It also contains quick-fix options

- Layer. This contains commands for working with different layers within an image

- Select. This contains commands for working with areas that have been selected within an image with one of the selection tools in the Toolbox

- Filter. This contains numerous filters that can be used to apply special effects to an image

- View. This contains commands for the size at which an image is displayed and also options for showing or hiding rulers and grid lines

- Window. This contains commands for how multiple images are displayed and also options for displaying all of the components of Elements

- Help. This contains the various Help options

Toolbox

The Toolbox contains tools for adding items to an image (such as shapes and text), selecting areas of an image and also for applying editing techniques. Some of the tools have more than one option, in which case they have a small black triangle at the bottom right of the default tool. To access additional tools in the Toolbox:

Click and hold here to access additional tools for a particular item

	Rectangular Marquee Tool	M
	Elliptical Marquee Tool	M

Default Toolbox tools:

The tools that have additional options are: the Marquee tools, the Lasso tools, the Object tools (i.e. the Rectangle tool), the Type tools, the Brush tools, the Eraser tools and the Stamp tools.

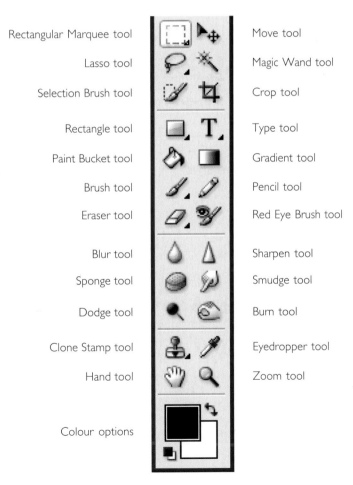

Left		Right
Rectangular Marquee tool		Move tool
Lasso tool		Magic Wand tool
Selection Brush tool		Crop tool
Rectangle tool		Type tool
Paint Bucket tool		Gradient tool
Brush tool		Pencil tool
Eraser tool		Red Eye Brush tool
Blur tool		Sharpen tool
Sponge tool		Smudge tool
Dodge tool		Burn tool
Clone Stamp tool		Eyedropper tool
Hand tool		Zoom tool
Colour options		

Shortcuts bar

The Shortcuts bar provides quick access to some of the most commonly used features within Elements. The Shortcuts bar is displayed by default and, if necessary, it can be hidden by selecting Window from the Menu bar and clicking on Shortcuts so that the tick next to it is removed. However, the only reason to do this is to create more space in the work area and in general the Shortcuts bar should be visible at all times.

PDF stands for Portable Document Format and it is a file format that has been developed by Adobe to enable files to be viewed on a variety of devices. PDF files also retain the exact formatting of the original document from which they were created.

Shortcuts bar items

Link to the Adobe website

Create New file

Browse for files using the File Browser

Save

Save as PDF

The Import button can be used to get images from digital cameras and scanners.

Open a file from your hard drive

Import a file from a different source

Save for the Web

Attach to an email

Link to online resources for Elements

Print

Step backward

Quick Fix options

Search for a Help topic

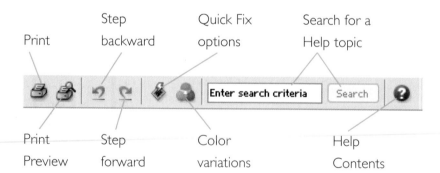

Enter search criteria   Search

Print Preview

Step forward

Color variations

Help Contents

Options bar

The Options bar provides attributes that can be set for a selected tool from the Toolbox. For instance, if the Eraser tool is selected, the Options bar offers choices for the type of eraser that can be used, its size, its mode and its opacity level. For each tool, a different set of options is available from the Options bar.

Using the Options bar

1 Click on a tool in the Toolbox (in this example it is the Brush tool)

If a tool has more than one option in the Toolbox, these are all displayed on the Options bar. Clicking on a different tool on the Options bar changes the currently selected tool in the Toolbox.

2 Select the options for the tool in the Options bar

3 Apply the tool to an image. The tool will maintain the settings in the Options bar until they are changed

Palettes

Elements uses palettes to group together similar editing functions and provide quick access to certain techniques. The available palettes are:

- Info. This displays information about the colour and position of an image or element within it

- Effects. This contains special effects that can be applied to an entire image or a selected part of an image

- How To. This offers advice on how to achieve particular digital imaging techniques

- Filters. This contains filters for more special effects. Each filter has its own dialog box in which settings can be applied and adjusted. Filters can be applied to an entire image or a selected part of an image

- Layers. This enables several layers to be included within an image. This can be useful if you want to add elements to an existing image, such as shapes or text. Layers can also be used to merge two separate images together

- Layer Styles. This provides different styles that can be applied to items on layers

- Swatches. This is a palette for selecting colours that can then be applied to parts of an image or elements that have been added to it

- Undo History. This can be used to undo all, or some, of the editing steps that have been performed. Every action that has been applied to an image is displayed in the Undo History palette and these actions can be reversed by dragging the slider at the side of the palette upwards

- Navigator. This can be used to move around an image and magnify certain areas of it

- Hints. This provides help information and guidance about a selected tool

To access palettes in the palette well, drag the cursor slowly over the palette names until the one you want is visible.

The Undo History palette can be used to revert to earlier stages of the editing process.

Working with palettes

By default all palettes are minimised and grouped in the palette well. However, it is possible to open one or more palettes so they're displayed independently from the palette well. To work with palettes:

1 Palettes are grouped together in the palette well at the top right of the work area

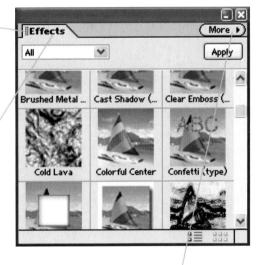

2 Click and drag here to move a palette away from the well (or move a detached palette back into the well)

Don't have too many palettes open at one time. If you do, the screen will become cluttered and it will be difficult to edit images effectively.

3 Click here on a palette in the well to view it once (when another selection is made the palette will return to the well)

4 Click here to view a palette's menu

5 Every palette has its own menu; its options depend on the functions within the palette

Preferences

A number of preferences can be set within Elements to determine the way the program operates. It is perfectly acceptable to leave all of the default settings as they are, but as you become more familiar with the program you may want to change some of the preference settings. Preferences can be accessed by selecting Edit>Preferences (Windows) from the Menu bar, and the available ones are:

In Mac OS X the Preferences menu can be accessed by selecting Photoshop Elements>Preferences from the Menu bar.

- General. This contains a variety of options for selecting items such as shortcut keys

- Saving Files. This determines the way Elements saves files

- Display & Cursors. This determines how cursors operate when certain tools are selected

- Transparency. This determines the colour, or transparency, of the background on which an open image resides

- Units & Rulers. This determines the unit of measurement used by items such as rulers

- Grid. This determines the colour and format of any grid

- Plug-Ins & Scratch Disks. This determines how Elements allocates disk space when processing editing tasks

- Memory & Image Cache. This determines how Elements allocates memory when processing editing tasks

Each preference has its own dialog box in which the specific preference settings can be made:

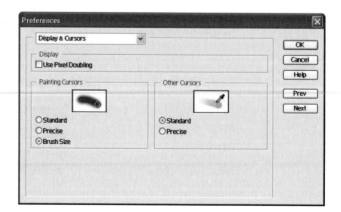

Display & Cursors Preferences

Getting help

One of the differences between Elements and the full version of Photoshop is the amount of assistance and guidance offered by each program. Since Photoshop is aimed more at the professional end of the market, the level of help is confined largely to the standard help directory that serves as an online manual. Elements also contains this, but in addition it has a number of items that are designed to take people through the digital image editing process as smoothly as possible. The two most important of these are the How To and the Hints palettes, which are looked at on the next page. There are also help items which can be accessed by selecting Help from the Menu bar, which includes online help, a glossary, tutorials and support details.

Using the online help files

Select Photoshop Elements Help from the Help menu and click Contents or Index. Then click once on an item to display it in the main window

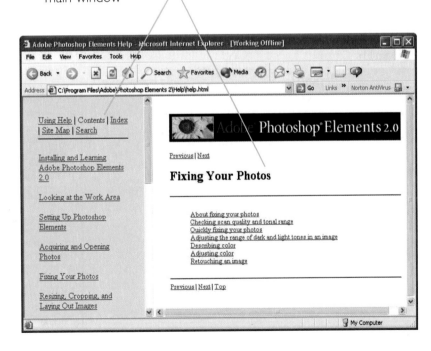

Using the How To palette

To use the How To palette:

1 Drag the How To palette from the palette well

2 Click here to access the How To palette categories

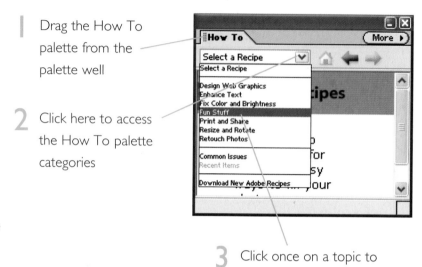

The Hints palette is a good way to work through some artistic techniques that can be created with Elements.

3 Click once on a topic to display a step-by-step guide

Using the Hints palette

To use the Hints palette:

1 Drag the Hints palette from the palette well

2 Select a tool from the Toolbox to view a description of its functions in the Hints palette

3 Click here to view information on related topics

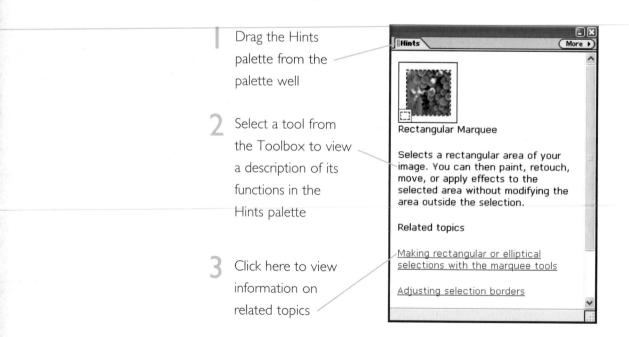

Working with images

This chapter shows you how to obtain and organise images, before you start manipulating them with image editing techniques.

Covers

Chapter Two

Obtaining images from cameras

The two main sources for obtaining digital images are digital cameras and scanners. With Elements, images can be opened directly from these devices.

In Mac OS X the camera software may have to be installed, before the camera is available from the Import menu.

Digital cameras

To obtain images from a digital camera, make sure the camera is turned on, connected to the computer and set to the Connect function. To download images:

1 Select File>Import from the Menu bar or click the Import button in the Shortcuts bar.

In Mac OS X, to open Elements automatically when a digital camera is connected to the computer, select Finder>Applications>Image Capture>Hot Play Action and choose Photoshop Elements as the required application.

2 Click here to select the device from which you want to download images

3 Click OK

If you are using Windows Me or XP you will be able to import images using Windows Image Acquisition (WIA) support which is available under WIA Support on the Import menu.

4 Select the image(s) you want to download and click Get Pictures. The selected image, or images, will then open as a new file, or files, in Elements

Once a device has been selected for the first time, it will then appear on the default Import menu.

Obtaining images from scanners

Scanners

One of the differences in capturing images with a scanner rather than a digital camera is that you can set the image resolution of the image in the scanner software, rather than just the physical size of the image. Once you have connected to your scanner (either from the Welcome screen or by selecting File>Import from the Menu bar and selecting the required scanner) a screen similar to this one will appear (depending on the scanner software):

Scanners can be thought of as flatbed digital cameras, in that they capture digital images on a similar type of image sensor.

I Enter details of the type of item you want to scan (this can include graphics and text as well as photographs) and click here for further options

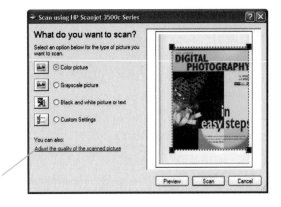

2 Enter a resolution value (use a setting of 150 or above for images that are going to be printed and a setting of 75 for images that are going to be used on the Web). Click OK in this screen and then click Scan on the previous one

A lot of scanners perform two scans on an image: the first one scans everything on the glass plate, then you can select the area you want to use and the next scan will capture this selection.

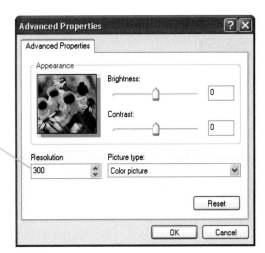

Grabbing video frames

A new feature in the latest version of Elements is the ability to capture still frames from digital video clips. To do this:

1 Select File>Import from the Menu bar (or click on the Import button in the Options bar) and select Frame From Video

PDF Image...
HP Scanjet 3500c Series...
Frame From Video...
WIA Support...

Some video frames can look blurred when they are stopped in the Frame From Video dialog box. Experiment with different frames to try and get the best image possible.

2 Click here to locate a video

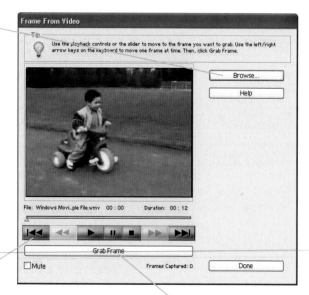

3 Use these controls to move through the video

Use the Pause button on the video controls panel to stop the video before you grab a frame.

4 Click here to grab the current video frame and click Done

5 The video frame is converted into a still image in Elements

Opening images

Once you have captured images with a digital camera or a scanner and stored them on your computer you can then open them in Elements. There are a number of options for this:

Open command

Images can also be opened by clicking on the Open button in the Shortcuts bar.

1 Select File>Open from the Menu bar or click the Open button in the Shortcuts bar:

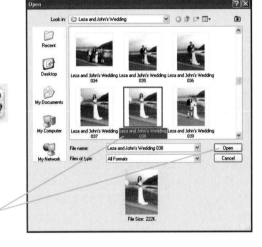

Another option for opening files is the Open Recent command, which is accessed from the File menu. This lists the files you have opened most recently.

2 Select an image from your hard drive and click Open

Open As command (Windows only)

This can be used to open a file in a different file format from its original format. To do this:

1 Select File>Open As from the Menu bar

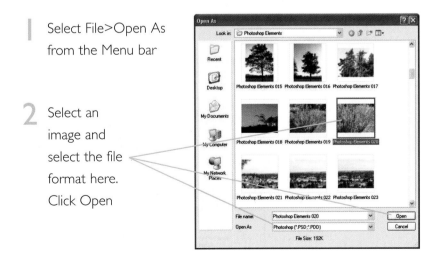

2 Select an image and select the file format here. Click Open

File Browser

The File Browser is another option for opening files. It can also be used to create new folders and rotate images.

Opening files

1 Select File>Browse from the Menu bar or click the Browse button in the Shortcuts bar:

The File Browser remains visible even when an image has been opened from it. This means that it is a good way to quickly open multiple images.

2 Locate the file you want to open in the File Browser and double-click on it to open it, or drag it into the work area

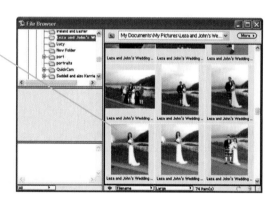

Displaying file information

1 Select File>Browse from the Menu bar

2 Locate a file and click once on it to display its details

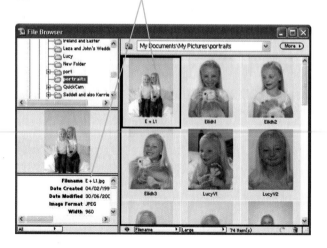

Creating new folders

1 Open the File Browser and click here to access its menu

2 Select New Folder from the menu to create a new folder within the currently selected one

3 Type a name for the new folder (the default name is already selected)

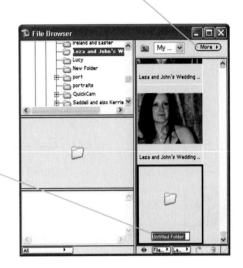

Rotating images

1 Select an image in the File Browser

When an image has been rotated in the File Browser, it has to be saved in Elements to effect the change.

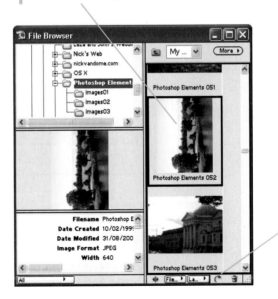

2 Click here to rotate the image

Creating new files

On some occasions it is useful to be able to open a new, blank file. This could be if you want to combine two or more images and you are not sure of the final size of the image, or if you have copied part of an image and you want to paste it into a new file. New files can also be useful for creating graphics from scratch, such as buttons for the Web. To create a new, blank file:

1 Select File>New from the Menu bar or click on the New button on the Shortcuts bar:

2 Enter the dimensions of the file and also its resolution, which will affect the size when it is printed

A resolution setting of 150 or above will ensure a high-quality printed image.

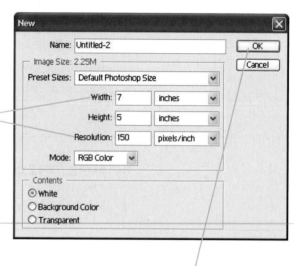

3 Click OK

4 The new, blank file is created and content can now be added to it

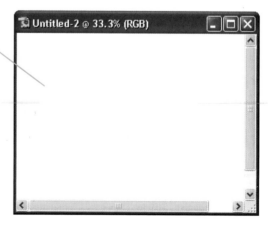

Saving images

File formats

When saving digital images, it is always a good idea to save them in at least two different file formats, particularly if layered elements such as text and shapes have been added. One of these formats should be the proprietary Photoshop format PSD or PDD. The reason that this should be used is that it will retain all of the layered information within an image. So if a text layer has been added, this will still be available for editing at a future date, once it has been saved and closed.

A proprietary file format is one that is specific to the program being used. It has greater flexibility when used within the program itself but cannot be distributed as easily as a JPEG or a GIF image can.

The other format that an image should be saved in is the one most appropriate for the use to which it is going to be put. Therefore, images that are going to be used on the Web should be saved as JPEG, GIF or PNG files, while an image that is going to be used for printing should be saved in a format such as TIFF. Once images have been saved in these formats, all of the layered information within them becomes flattened into a single layer and it will not be possible to edit this once the image has been saved. By default, images are saved in the same format as the one in which they were opened. Most image formats have dialog boxes for options when they are being saved, like this one for JPEGs:

Another print format is EPS (Photoshop EPS in Elements) which is sometimes used by commercial printers.

In the JPEG Options dialog, the file size is displayed and also the download time over the Web at a given setting

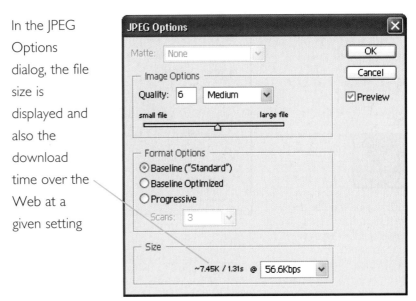

Save and Save As

To save new and existing images after they have been edited:

The Save As command should be used if you want to make a copy of an image with a different file name. Editing changes can then be made to the copy, while the original remains untouched.

1 Select File>Save (or Save As) from the Menu bar or click the Save button in the Shortcuts bar.

2 Click here in the Save As dialog box to select a file format

By default, the Save As command saves an image in the same format as the one in which it was opened.

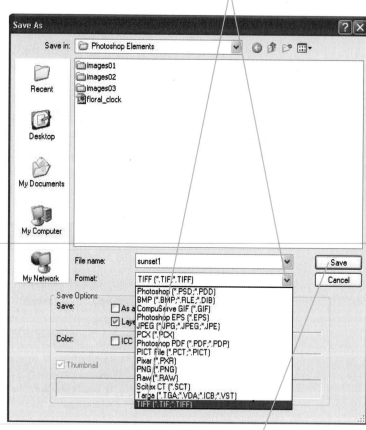

If a new image (i.e. one created using the File> New command) is being saved for the first time, it will be done in the Elements proprietary format, unless specified otherwise.

3 Click Save

Batch renaming

As you obtain more and more images you may find that they have very similar names, particularly if they have been downloaded directly from a digital camera. By default, they will be named sequentially as DCP123 etc. In instances like this, the File Browser can be used to rename entire folders of images. To do this:

1 Select File>Browse from the Menu bar to open the File Browser

2 Select a folder or individual files you want to rename

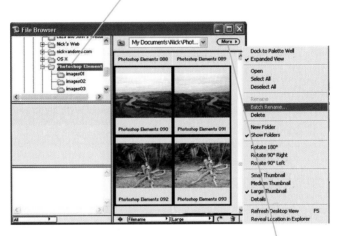

 Even with batch renaming, images will have the same base name. However, it should be a more meaningful one than the default name used when images are downloaded from a digital camera.

4 Click here to select a destination folder for the renamed images

3 Click here to access the File Browser menu and select Batch Rename

 If you want the renamed files to remain in the original folder, check on the 'Rename in same folder' button in the Batch Rename dialog box.

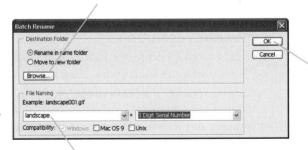

6 Click OK

5 Enter the base name for the images to be renamed

Image size

The physical size of a digital image can sometimes be a confusing issue as it is frequently dealt with under the term 'resolution'. Unfortunately, resolution can be applied to a number of areas of digital imaging: image resolution, monitor resolution, print size and print resolution.

Image resolution

The resolution of an image is determined by the number of pixels in it. This is counted as a vertical and a horizontal value i.e. 640 x 480. When multiplied together it gives the overall resolution i.e. 307,200 pixels in this case. This is frequently the headline figure quote by digital camera manufacturers e.g. 2 million pixels (or 2 megapixels). To view the image resolution in Elements:

To view an image on a monitor at its actual size or the size at which it will currently be printed, select the Zoom tool from the Toolbox and select Actual Pixels or Print Size from the Options bar.

1. Select Image>Resize>Image Size from the Menu bar

2. The image size is displayed here (in pixels)

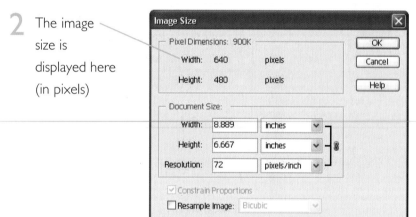

The Resolution figure under the Document Size heading is used to determine the size at which the image will be printed. If this is set to 72, then the onscreen size and the printed size should be roughly the same.

Monitor resolution

Most modern computer monitors display digital images at between 72–96 pixels per inch (ppi). This means that every inch of the screen contains approximately this number of pixels. So for an image being displayed at 100%, the onscreen size will be the number of pixels horizontally divided by 72 (or 96 depending on the monitor) and the same vertically. In the above example this would mean the image would be viewed at 9 inches by 6.5 inches approximately.

Document size (print resolution)

Pixels in an image are not a set size, which means that images can be printed at a variety of sizes, simply by contracting or expanding the available pixels. This is done by changing the resolution in the Document Size section of the Image Size dialog box. (When dealing with document size, think of this as the size of the printed document.) To set the size at which an image will be printed:

The higher the print resolution, the better the final printed image. Aim for a minimum of 150 pixels per inch for the best printed output.

1 Select Image>Resize>Image Size from the Menu bar

To work out the size at which an image will be printed, divide the pixel dimensions (height and width) by the resolution value under the Document Size heading.

2 Change the resolution here (or change the Width and Height of the image). Make sure the Resample Image box is checked off

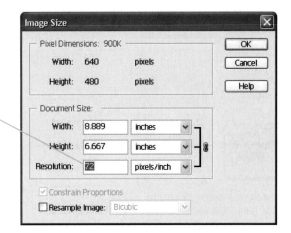

The print resolution determines how many pixels are used in each inch of the printed image. However, the number of coloured dots used to represent each pixel on the paper is determined by the printer resolution, measured in dots per inch (dpi). So if the print resolution is 72 ppi and the printer resolution is 2880 dpi, each pixel will be represented by 40 coloured dots i.e. 2880 divided by 72.

3 By changing one value, the other two are updated automatically. Click OK

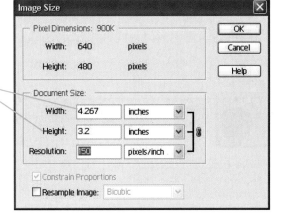

Resampling images

The process of adding pixels to an image to increase its size is known as 'interpolation'.

All digital images can be increased or decreased in size. This involves adding or removing pixels from the image. Decreasing the size of an image is relatively straightforward and involves removing redundant pixels. However, increasing the size of an image involves adding pixels by digital guesswork. To do this, Elements looks at the existing pixels and works out the best nearest match for the ones that are to be added. Increasing or decreasing the size of a digital image is known as 'resampling'.

Resampling

Since it involves digital guesswork by Elements, resampling up results in inferior image quality.

Resampling down decreases the size of the image and it is more effective than sampling up. To do this:

1 Select Image>Resize>Image Size from the Menu bar

2 Check on the Resample Image box

To keep the same resolution for an image, resample it by changing the pixel dimensions' height and width. To keep the same Document Size (e.g. the size at which it will be printed) resample it by changing the resolution.

3 Resample the image by changing the pixel dimensions, the height and width or the resolution

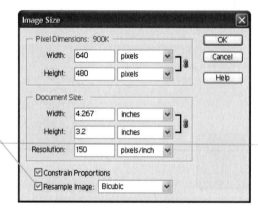

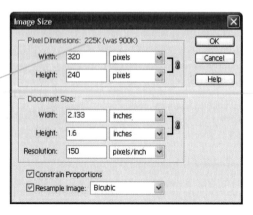

Make sure the Constrain Proportions box is checked on if you want the image to be increased or decreased in size proportionally, rather than just one value being altered.

4 Changing any of the values above alters the physical size of the image. Click OK

First digital steps

This chapter shows you how to get up and running with digital image editing and details some effective editing techniques.

Covers

Chapter Three

Colour enhancements

Some of the simplest but most effective editing changes that can be made to digital images are colour enhancements. These can help to transform a mundane image into a stunning one and Elements offers a variety of methods for achieving this. Some of these are verging towards the professional end of image editing while others are done almost automatically by Elements. These are known as Auto adjustments and some simple manual adjustments can also be made to the brightness and contrast of an image. All of these colour enhancement features can be accessed from the Enhance menu on the Menu bar.

Auto Levels

This automatically adjusts the overall colour tone in an image in relation to the lightest and darkest points in the image:

If you do not like the colour enhancement once it has been applied to the image, click on the Step Backward button on the Shortcuts bar.

Auto Contrast

This automatically adjusts the contrast in an image:

Auto Color Correction

This automatically adjusts all the colour elements within an image:

Apply small amounts of Brightness and Contrast at a time when you are editing an image. This will help ensure that the end result does not look too unnatural.

Adjust Brightness/Contrast

This can be used to manually adjust the brightness and contrast in an image:

1 Select Enhance>Adjust Brightness/Contrast>Brightness/Contrast from the Menu bar

2 Drag these sliders to adjust the image brightness and contrast

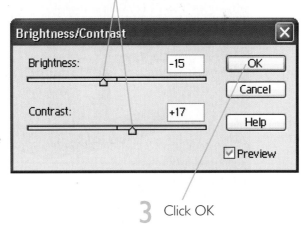

Always make sure that the Preview box is ticked when you are applying colour enhancements. This will display the changes as you make them and before they are applied to the image.

3 Click OK

Cropping

Cropping is a technique that can be used to remove unwanted areas of an image and highlight the main subject. The area to be cropped can only be selected as a rectangle. To crop an image:

Very few photographic images are perfect without editing. Cropping should be considered as standard for most images.

1   Select the Crop tool from the Toolbox:

2   Click and drag on an image to select the area to be cropped. The area that is selected is retained and the area to be cropped appears greyed-out

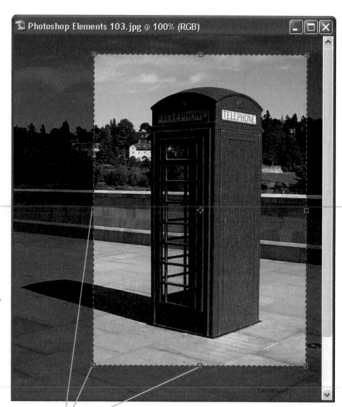

The Crop command can also be verified by clicking on the tick button in the Options bar once a crop area has been selected.

3   Click and drag here to resize the crop area

4   Press Return or Enter to crop the image

Cloning

Cloning is a technique that can be used to copy one area of an image over another. This can be used to cover up small imperfections in an image, such as a dust mark or a spot, and also to copy or remove large items in an image such as a person.

To clone items:

If you are copying a large object with cloning, do not release the mouse once you have started dragging the cursor for the cloning process; otherwise, the cloned image will be incomplete.

1 Select the Clone Stamp tool from the Toolbox:

2 Set the Clone Stamp tool options in the Options bar

When you are removing large objects by cloning over them, you will probably have to move your source point several times. This will ensure that there is smooth coverage over the cloned item.

3 Hold down Alt and click on the image to select a source point from which the cloning will start

4 Drag the cursor to copy everything over which the cursor passes

Pattern cloning

The Pattern Stamp tool can be used to copy a selected pattern over an image, or a selected area of an image. To do this:

The Pattern Stamp tool is grouped in the Toolbox with the Clone Stamp tool. It can be selected from the Options bar or by clicking and holding on the black triangle in the corner of the Clone Stamp tool and then selecting the Pattern Stamp tool from the subsequent list.

1 Select the Pattern Stamp tool from the Toolbox:

2 Click here in the Options bar to select a pattern

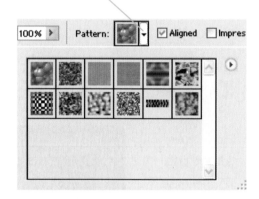

3 Click and drag on an image to copy the selected pattern over it

Patterns can be added to the patterns palette by selecting an image, or an area of an image, and selecting Edit> Define Pattern from the Menu bar. Then give the pattern a name in the Pattern Name dialog box and click OK.

Rotating

Various rotation commands can be applied to images and also individual layers in layered images. This can be useful for positioning items and also for correcting the orientation of an image that is on its side or upside down.

Rotating a whole image

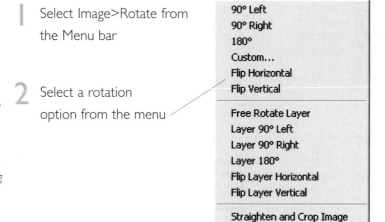

| 1 | Select Image>Rotate from the Menu bar |

Rotation options are also available in the Quick Fix dialog box which can be accessed by selecting Enhance>Quick Fix from the Menu bar or by clicking on the Quick Fix button on the Shortcuts bar.

| 2 | Select a rotation option from the menu |

90° Left
90° Right
180°
Custom...
Flip Horizontal
Flip Vertical

Free Rotate Layer
Layer 90° Left
Layer 90° Right
Layer 180°
Flip Layer Horizontal
Flip Layer Vertical

Straighten and Crop Image
Straighten Image

| 3 | Select Custom to enter your own value for the amount you want an image rotated |

If an image is only slightly misaligned, then only a small angle figure is required in the Rotate Canvas dialog box. A figure of 1 or 2 can sometimes be sufficient.

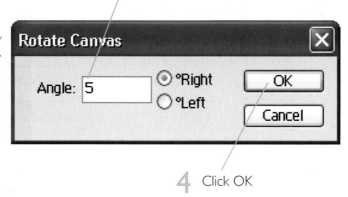

| 4 | Click OK |

Rotating a layer

If an image is made up of two or more layers, these can be rotated independently from one another. To rotate a layer:

For more information about working with layers, see Chapter Seven.

1   Select an image that consists of two or more layers. Select one of the layers

2   Select Image>Rotate from the Menu bar

| 90° Left |
| 90° Right |
| 180° |
| Custom... |
| Flip Horizontal |
| Flip Vertical |
| Free Rotate Layer |
| Layer 90° Left |
| Layer 90° Right |
| Layer 180° |
| Flip Layer Horizontal |
| Flip Layer Vertical |
| Straighten and Crop Image |
| Straighten Image |

3   Select a layer rotation option from the menu

4   The selected layer is rotated independently from the rest of the image

Free rotation

The rotate menu can also be used to rotate an item manually. This is done by rotating individual layers. If no layers have been added to an image, the image is converted into a layer so that it can be rotated. To apply free rotation:

1   Select Image>Rotate>Free Rotate Layer from the Menu bar

By default, images are opened with no regular layers, just the background layer, which is locked.

2   If the image has no additional layers, i.e. it is a background or locked layer, a dialog box will appear asking if you want to convert the background into a regular layer. Click OK

3   Enter the details for the new layer and click OK

4   Click near the image border and drag to rotate manually

Once an image has been rotated, the image canvas is visible beneath it from where it has been rotated.

Transforming

The Transform commands can be used to resize an image and to apply some basic distortion techniques. These commands can be accessed by selecting Image>Transform from the Menu bar.

Free Transform
This enables you to manually alter the size of an image. To do this:

When any of the Transform commands are applied, the image has to be converted into a layer. After Step 1, you will be asked if you want to convert the current background image into a layer. Click OK and give the layer a name in the New Layer dialog box.

1 Select Image>Transform>FreeTransform from the Menu bar

2 Click and drag here to transform the vertical size of the image

3 Click and drag here to transform the horizontal size of the image

The Free Transform option is best used if you want to create unusual effects by changing the dimensions of an image. If you want to accurately resize an image, use the Image> Resize>Image Size option on the Menu bar.

4 Click and drag here to transform the vertical and horizontal size of the image. Hold down Shift to transform it in proportion

Skew

This enables you to manually slant an image. To do this:

1 Select Image>Transform>Skew from the Menu bar

2 Click and drag here to skew the image horizontally

All the Transform functions are applied or discarded by clicking a tick or a circle with a line through it respectively. Both of these appear on the Options bar.

3 Click and drag here to skew the image vertically

4 Click and drag here to skew the image vertically and horizontally. Hold down Shift to skew it in proportion

Distort

This enables you to manually stretch an image. To do this:

1 Select Image>Transform>Distort from the Menu bar

2 Click and drag here to distort the image along the horizontal axis

3 Click and drag here to distort the image along the vertical axis

4 Click and drag here to distort the image along the vertical and horizontal axis

Perspective

This enables you to change the perspective of an image, to give it an elongated effect. To do this:

1 Select Image>Transform>Perspective from the Menu bar

2 Click and drag here to change the vertical and horizontal perspective of the image

The Perspective function is a good one to apply to buildings: it can make them look a lot taller, like skyscrapers reaching into the distance.

3 Click and drag here to change the vertical perspective

4 Click and drag here to change the horizontal perspective

Magnification

There are a number of ways in Elements in which the magnification at which an image is being viewed can be increased or decreased. This can be useful if you want to zoom in on a particular part of an image, for editing purposes, or if you want to view a whole image to see the result of editing effects that have been applied.

View menu

The View menu can be used to display rulers at the top and left of an image, which can be useful for precise measurement and placement. There is also a command for displaying a grid over the top of the whole image.

Select View from the Menu bar and select one of the options from the View menu

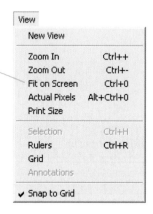

Zoom tool

Click and drag with the Zoom tool over a small area to increase the magnification to the maximum i.e. 1600%. This can be particularly useful when performing close-up editing tasks such as removing red-eye.

Select the Zoom tool from the Toolbox and click once on an image to enlarge it (usually by 100% each time). Hold down Alt and click to decrease the magnification

Navigator palette

This can be used to move around an image and also magnify certain areas. To use the Navigator palette:

1 Click and drag here to detach the Navigator palette from the palette well

The Navigator palette also has buttons for zooming in and out. These are located at the left and right of the slider.

2 Drag this slider to magnify the area of the image within the red rectangle

3 Drag the rectangle to change the area of the image that is being magnified

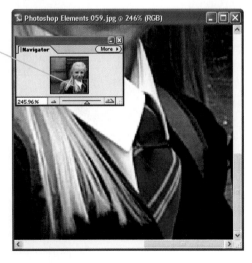

Burn and dodge

Burn and dodge are two traditional photographic techniques for darkening (burn) or lightening (dodge) areas of an image. In Elements there are tools in the Toolbox for achieving these effects. To do this:

The Burn and Dodge tools can be used on a whole image, or a selection can be made within the image and the tools used within the selection. In this case, only the pixels within the selected area will be affected by the tools.

1 The original image

Options for the Burn and Dodge tools can be selected on the Options bar once the tools have been selected.

2 Select the Burn tool from the Toolbox and drag it over an area of an image to darken it

3 Select the Dodge tool from the Toolbox and drag it over an area of an image to lighten it

Sponge

The Sponge tool is used in a similar way to the Burn and Dodge tools, except that it increases or decreases the colour saturation of the area over which it is applied. To use the Sponge tool:

1 Select the Sponge tool in the Toolbox and click here in the Options bar to select Saturate or Desaturate

2 Drag the Sponge tool over the image, or an area of the image, to achieve the desired effect

The saturation of a colour is the intensity at which that colour is displayed.

Eraser

The Eraser tool can be used to remove areas of an image. It also has options that can be used to erase areas of an image when it has been created using layers. To use the standard Eraser tool:

If the opacity setting in the Options bar is less than 100% then the area that is erased will be transparent to a greater or lesser degree.

1 Select the Eraser tool from the Toolbox:

2 Select the required options from the Options bar

The other Eraser options are the Background Eraser and the Magic Eraser. The Background Eraser can be used to remove areas around a main subject and the Magic Eraser can be used to remove large areas of similar colour.

3 Click and drag to remove an area of an image

Quick wins for digital images

In digital image editing, there are a number of techniques and effects that can be used to quickly and significantly enhance images. This chapter looks at some of these 'quick wins' and shows how they can be applied to images.

Covers

Chapter Four

Removing red-eye

The best way to deal with red-eye is to avoid it in the first place. Try using a camera that has a red-eye reduction function. This uses an extra flash, just before the picture is taken, to diminish the effect of red-eye.

One of the most common problems with photographs of people, whether they are taken digitally or with a film-based camera, is red-eye. This is caused when the camera's flash is used and then reflects in the subject's pupils. This can create the dreaded red-eye effect, when the subject can unintentionally be transformed into a demonic character. Unless you have access to professional studio lighting equipment or have a removable flash unit that can be positioned away from the subject's face, then sooner or later you will capture images that contain red-eye.

Elements has recognised that removing red-eye is one of the top priorities for most amateur photographers and a specific tool for this purpose has been included in the Toolbox: the Red Eye Brush tool. To use this:

1 Open an image that contains red-eye

You can also use the Red Eye Brush tool (using the same red-eye technique) to recolour other small areas within an image.

2 Select the Zoom tool from the Toolbox:

3 Click on the affected area until it is at a suitable level
of magnification

*If you zoom in to
a sufficient
magnification
(800% or above)
each individual
pixel can be recoloured using the
Pen tool from the Toolbox.
However, this will not give as
subtle an effect as the Red Eye
Brush tool.*

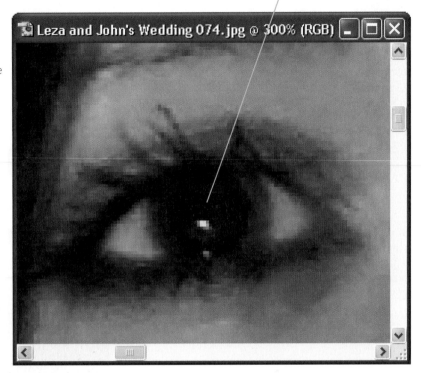

4 Select the Red eye Brush tool from the Toolbox:

5 Click here in the Options bar to select the brush type and size

For removing red-eye, select a very small brush size. Otherwise too
large an area may be recoloured, which could make the eye look
unnaturally large.

If the current colour is selected by using First Click in the Sampling box, the colour will be selected each time you click on the image. If it is selected by using Current Color, this will be the colour in the Current box. To change this, click on the colour box and select a new colour with the Color Picker.

6 Click here in the Options bar to select how the current colour (i.e. the one to be replaced) is to be selected

7 Click here in the Options bar to select a replacement colour

8 Select a replacement colour from the Color Picker and click OK

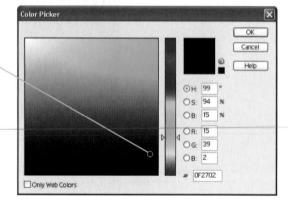

The tolerance level determines how closely matched, in terms of colour, adjacent pixels have to be in order for the replacement colour to be applied to them. A high tolerance includes a wider range of colours and vice versa.

9 Click here in the Options bar to select the tolerance level by dragging the slider

10 Click on individual pixels to change the current colour to the replacement one

The replacement colour will blend with the current one to create the final colour. Each click will increase the saturation of the new colour.

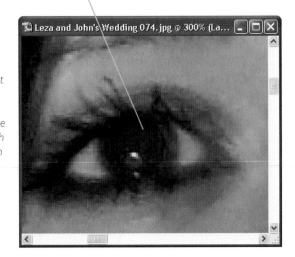

11 View at 100% magnification to ensure that all of the red-eye has been removed

Straightening images

If you use scanned images, you will quickly discover that it can be difficult to capture a perfectly straight image. Invariably, scanned images appear at a slight angle once the scanning process has been completed, regardless of how careful you are when you place the original image in the scanner. As shown in Chapter Three, images can be rotated manually, but there is also a function for straightening images in one operation. This can be used to not only straighten images, but also to crop them at the same time. To straighten an image:

When scanning images it is best not to spend too much time trying to get the image straight. This is because it can be a frustrating process and also because of the ease with which Elements can cure the problem.

1 Open the image that requires to be straightened

2 Select Image>Rotate> Straighten Image from the Menu bar

3 The image is straightened within the orientation of the image. There is also a border around the whole image as a result of this process

To straighten and crop an image:

1 Open the image that requires to be straightened and cropped

Once they have been straightened images can also be cropped manually using the Crop tool in the Toolbox.

2 In the Menu bar, select Image>Rotate> Straighten and Crop Image

3 The image is straightened and cropped so that the border visible after straightening is removed

Quick Fix options

The Quick Fix options in Elements offer a number of functions within the one location. This makes it easier to apply a number of techniques at the same time. To access the Quick Fix options, select Enhance>Quick Fix from the Menu bar. The Quick Fix options cover four categories of digital image editing:

The Quick Fix options can also be accessed by clicking on the Quick Fix button in the Shortcuts bar.

Brightness

Click here to access the Brightness category

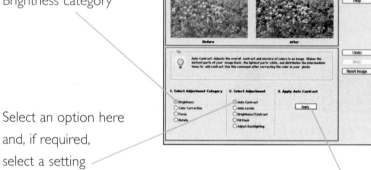

Several options can be applied sequentially, without having to leave the Quick Fix dialog box. Click the Apply button after each effect has been selected.

Select an option here and, if required, select a setting

Click Apply to preview the changes and OK to apply them to the image

Color Correction

Click here to access the Color Correction category

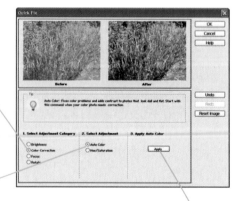

The Quick Fix options can also be selected individually from the Enhance and Image menus.

Select an option here and, if required, select a setting

Click Apply to preview the changes and OK to apply them to the image

Focus

The Sharpen tool in the Toolbox can also be used to improve the focus of an image. The Blur tool can also be used to blur images or selections within them.

1 Click here to access the Focus category

Using the Auto Focus option will only improve the focus of an image slightly. It will not bring a very out-of-focus image into perfect sharpness.

2 Select an option here and, if required, select a setting

3 Click Apply to preview the changes and OK to apply them to the image

Rotate

1 Click here to access the Rotate category

The Rotate options do not have settings that can be selected in the Apply Rotation section in the Quick Fix dialog box, only Apply.

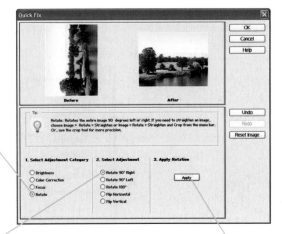

2 Select an option here

3 Click Apply to preview the changes and OK to apply them to the image

Variations

The Variations option is a quick way to see how an image will look with varying amounts of different colours applied to it. To do this:

1 Open an image and click on the Color Variations button in the Options bar:

2 Select a colour variation to use for the image. The selection is displayed in 'After' at the top of the illustration

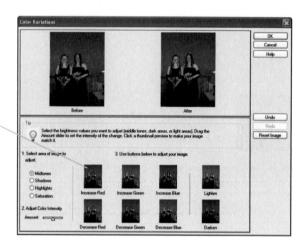

To apply a greater amount of each variation, click on the selected thumbnail several times.

3 Select an area of the image to adjust

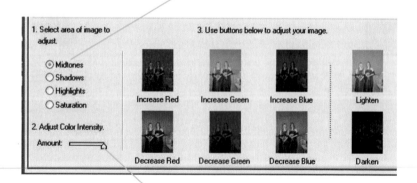

4 Drag this slider to increase or decrease the amount of adjustment that is applied

Creating greyscale images

Most digital cameras and scanners are capable of converting colour images into greyscale at the point of capture. However, it is also possible to use Elements to convert existing colour images into greyscale ones. To do this:

The term 'greyscale' refers to a range of grey shades between white and black.

1 Open a colour image and select Image>Mode> Grayscale from the Menu bar

When creating greyscale images, make a copy of the original first. Use the copy to create the greyscale image.

2 In the subsequent dialog box, click OK to remove the colour information from the image

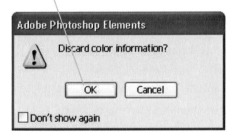

3 The image is converted into greyscale. Some colour adjustment editing can then be done to it, but this is more limited than for colour images e.g. Auto Color Correction is not available

Panoramas

Creating panoramas

For anyone who takes landscape pictures the desire to create a panorama occurs sooner or later. With film-based cameras, this usually involves sticking several photographs together to create the panorama, albeit a rather patchwork one. With digital images the end result can look a lot more professional and Elements has a dedicated function for achieving this: Photomerge.

When creating a panorama there are a few rules to follow:

Do not include too many images in a panorama, otherwise it could be too large for viewing or printing easily.

- If possible, use a tripod to ensure that your camera stays at the same level for all of the shots

- Keep the same exposure settings for all images

- Make sure that there is a reasonable overlap between images (about 20%). Some cameras enable you to align the correct overlap between the images

- Keep the same distance between yourself and the object you are capturing. Otherwise the end result will look out of perspective

To create a panorama:

1. Capture the images that you want to use in the panorama and save them to your hard drive:

Photoshop Elements 021   Photoshop Elements 022   Photoshop Elements 023

2. Select File>Create Photomerge from the Menu bar

3 Click Browse to locate the images you want to use

4 Select the files and click Open

Panoramas do not just have to be of landscapes. They can also be used for items such as a row of buildings or crowds at a sporting event.

5 In the Photomerge dialog box the source files are displayed. Click OK to create the panorama

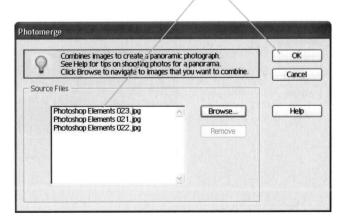

The tools at the top left of the Photomerge box can be used to (from top to bottom) Select, Rotate, Set Vanishing Point, Zoom or Move the panorama.

6 The panorama is created automatically and displayed in the Photomerge dialog box

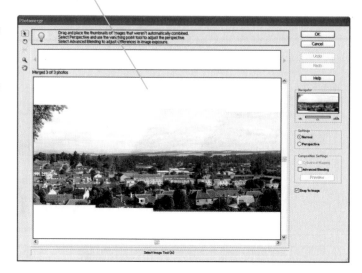

Click on the Cylindrical Mapping check box under Composition Settings to create a 3-D barrel effect for the panorama. This is only available if the Perspective radio button has been selected.

7 Click OK to create the final image

8 If required, crop the image to remove any uneven edges

Click on the Advanced Blending box under Composition Settings to adjust any differences in exposure in the individual images.

Non-sequential panoramas

Panoramas of images that are not in sequence are created in a similar way to sequential ones, except that the process is less automated. To create a non-sequential panorama, complete the first four steps for creating a panorama, then:

1 A warning box appears stating that the images cannot be created as a panorama. Click OK

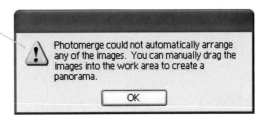

Photomerge could not automatically arrange any of the images. You can manually drag the images into the work area to create a panorama.

OK

Apply any editing changes, such as colour correction and cropping, to images before they are added to a collage. Some editing will probably also be required on the final image, but try and lessen the amount of work at this stage by preparing the images initially.

2 Drag the images into the Photomerge work area to create the panorama. Position them manually to create the required image

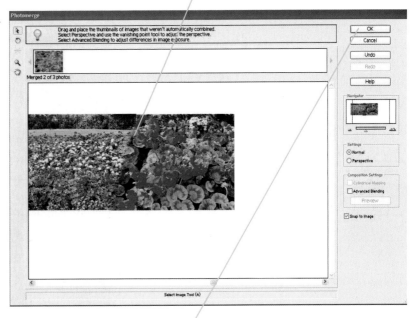

3 Click OK to create the final image

Improving lighting

One of the most delicate issues for any type of photography is lighting. If the lighting is wrong, a wonderful photographic opportunity can be lost. Two of the most common lighting problems are:

- Dark subject against a bright background (i.e. the subject is in shade because the light source is behind them)

- Overexposed backgrounds

Both of these problems can be solved in Elements through the use of the Adjust Lighting features.

Fill Flash

Fill Flash is a photographic technique where flash is used even though there is enough light to capture the image. This is used when the light source is behind the subject. Flash is then applied to lighten the subject and compensate for the light behind it. In Elements the same effect can be achieved through digital means. To do this:

Fill Flash can be applied to an entire image, but the same effect can be achieved by adjusting the brightness. The most effective use of Fill Flash is on a selection within an image.

For more information on selecting items, see Chapter Six.

1 Open an image which has the main subject in shadow

2 Select the main subject

...cont'd

3 Select Enhance>Adjust Lighting>Fill Flash from the Menu bar

4 Drag this slider to lighten the selection. Check on Preview to see the effect

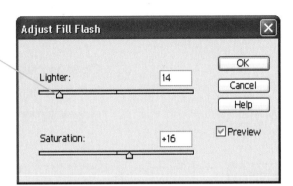

To avoid the need to use the Fill Flash function in Elements, always use a flash when you are capturing images of a subject where the light source is directly behind them.

5 Click OK to apply the Fill Flash effect

Use the Saturation slider in the Adjust Fill Flash dialog box to increase the intensity of colour in the selected area, if it has become too pale as a result of the lighten effect.

Backlighting

Backlighting is a similar effect to Fill Flash, except that it is applied to a background that is too bright and therefore appears washed-out. To apply backlighting:

1 Open an image with a washed-out background

2 Select the background

3 Select Enhance>Adjust Lighting>Adjust Backlighting from the Menu bar

4 Drag this slider to darken the background

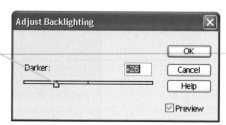

5 Click OK to apply the effect

Beyond the basics

Since Elements is based on the full version of Photoshop, it contains a number of powerful features for precise image editing. This chapter looks at some of these features and shows how you can take your image editing skills to the next level.

Covers

Chapter Five

Hue and saturation

The hue and saturation command can be used to edit the colour elements of an image. However, they work slightly differently from commands such as those for the brightness and contrast. There are three areas that are covered by the hue and saturation command: colour, colour strength and lightness. To adjust the hue and saturation of an image:

1 Open an image

By altering the hue of an image some interesting abstract colour effects can be created. This can be very effective if you are producing several versions of the same image, such as for a poster.

2 Select Enhance>Adjust Color>Hue/ Saturation from the Menu bar

3 Drag this slider to adjust the Hue of an image i.e. change the colours in the image

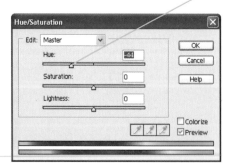

4 Drag this slider to adjust the Saturation i.e. the intensity of colours in the image

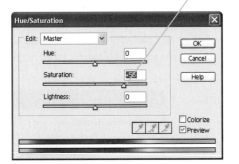

The Lightness option is similar to adjusting image brightness.

5 Check on the Colorize box to create a duotone image

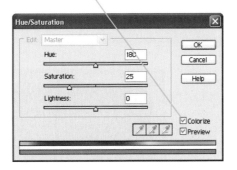

6 Click OK to apply any changes that have been made

Histogram

The histogram is a device that displays the tonal range of the pixels in an image and it can be used for very precise editing of an image. The histogram (Image>Histogram) is depicted in a graph format and it displays how the pixels in an image are distributed across the image, from the darkest (black) to the lightest (white) points. Another way of considering the histogram is that it displays the values of an image's highlights, midtones and shadows:

The tonal range (level) of an image, as displayed in the histogram, varies between 0–255.

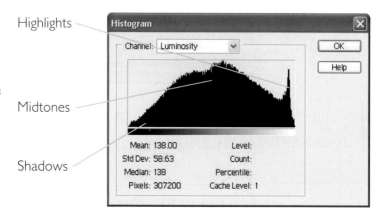

The histogram graph corresponds to the tonal range of the highlights, midtones and shadows in an image:

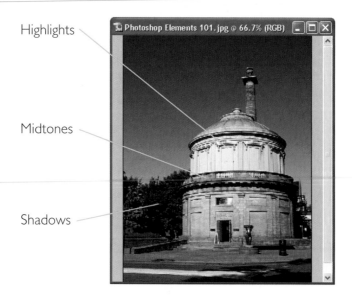

Ideally, the histogram graph should show a reasonably consistent range of tonal distribution, indicating an image that has good contrast and detail:

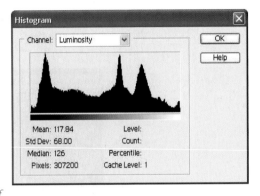

The histogram works by looking at the individual colour channels of an image (Red, Green, Blue, also known as the RGB colour model) or at a combination of all three, which is displayed as the Luminosity in the Channel box.

However, if the tonal range is bunched at one end of the graph, this indicates that the image is underexposed or overexposed:

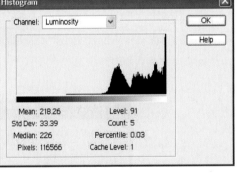

Overexposure

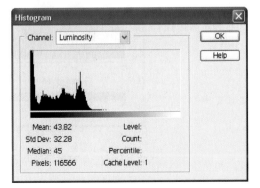

Underexposure

Levels

While the histogram displays the tonal range of an image, the Levels function can be used to edit this range. Any changes made using the Levels function will then be visible in the histogram. Levels allow you to redistribute pixels between the darkest and lightest points in an image, and also to set these point manually if you want. To use the Levels function:

The Levels function can be used to adjust the tonal range of a specific area of an image by first making a selection and then using the Levels dialog box. For more details on selecting areas see Chapter Six.

1 Open an image

In the Levels dialog box, the graph is the same as the one shown in the histogram.

2 Select Enhance>Adjust Brightness/Contrast>Levels from the Menu bar

Image shadows, midtones and highlights can be altered by dragging the markers for the black, midtone and white input points.

Midtone input point

Black input point

White input point

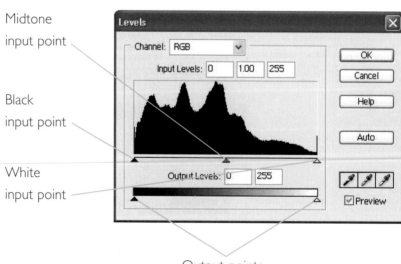

Output points

3 Drag the black point and the white point sliders to the first pixels denoted in the graph to increase the contrast

It is worth adjusting an image's black and white points before any other editing is performed.

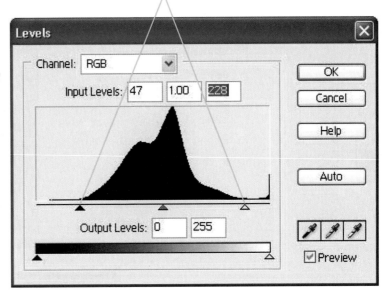

Move the midtones point slider to darken or lighten the midtones in an image.

4 Drag the output sliders towards the middle to decrease the contrast

The Auto button in the Levels dialog box produces the same effect as using the Enhance>Auto Levels command from the Menu bar.

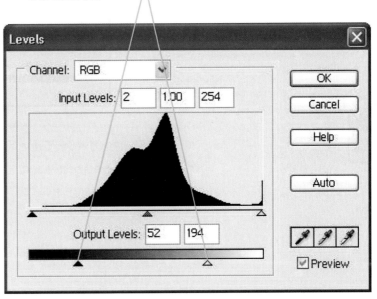

Pegging black and white points

Since Levels works by distributing pixels between the black and white points of an image, it makes sense to define these points for each image. This can be done by using the eyedroppers in the Levels dialog box:

With an image open, access the Levels dialog box by selecting Enhance>Adjust Brightness/Contrast>Levels from the Menu bar

The Info palette can be used to see the colour values of the areas selected for the black, white and grey points.

2 Click on the Set Black Point eyedropper and click on the image's darkest point to set the black point

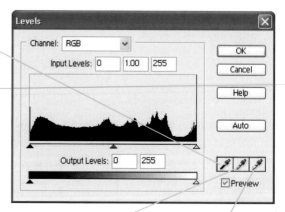

To set a white point, use an area that is coloured white, rather than a burnt out area of an image.

If the colour in an image does not look right after setting the black, grey and white points, try selecting different areas of colour with the relevant eyedroppers.

3 Click on the Set Grey Point eyedropper and click on a grey area to set the grey point

4 Click on the Set White Point eyedropper and click on the image's lightest point to set the white point

Equalize

The Equalize function works in a similar way to adjusting the Levels of an image, in that it redistributes the pixels in an image to try and achieve a more consistent level of brightness throughout the image. To equalize an image:

1 Open an image

2 Select Image>Adjustments>Equalize from the Menu bar

3 Colour is equalized across the image

Invert

The Invert function creates a negative effect for an image. To invert an image:

| Open an image

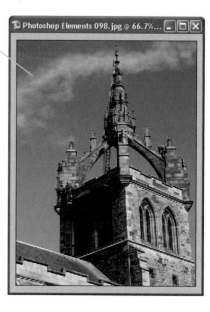

The negative effect produced by the Invert function on a colour image is not exactly the same as a film negative. However, if it is applied to a black and white image it is almost the same as a genuine black and white negative.

2 Select Image>Adjustments>Invert from the Menu bar

3 The negative of the image is displayed

Posterize

The Posterize function reduces the number of colours used in an image, to create a more abstract appearance. To posterize an image:

1. Open an image

2. Select Image>Adjustments>Posterize from the Menu bar

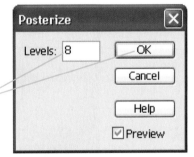

3. Enter a figure for the number of colour levels to be used. Click OK

4. The number of colour levels in the image is reduced accordingly

Sharpening

Sharpening is a technique that can be used to improve the definition of a slightly blurred image. It does this by emphasising the contrast between adjacent pixels. The full range of sharpening options is available from the Filter>Sharpen menu on the Menu bar and there is also a Sharpen tool in the Toolbox. To use this:

For more precise sharpening, use the Unsharp Mask which can be accessed by selecting Filter>Sharpen> Unsharp Mask from the Menu bar. This activates a dialog box that can be used to apply settings for specific aspects of the sharpening process.

1 Select the Sharpen tool in the Toolbox and make the required selections in the Options bar

2 Drag the Sharpen tool over an image to apply the effect

If too much sharpening is applied the affected area could appear almost serrated since the lines between adjacent pixels will become too noticeable, as is the case with this example.

Sharpening is useful for images that are going to be printed: it's more forgiving than viewing images online.

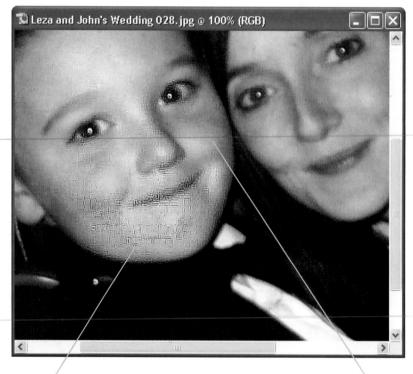

With sharpening applied   Without sharpening

Selecting areas

The true power of digital image editing comes into its own when you are able to select areas of an image and edit them independently from the rest of the image. This chapter looks at the various ways that selections can be made with Elements and shows how to edit individual selections.

Covers

Chapter Six

About selections

One of the most important aspects of image editing is the ability to select areas within an image. This can be used in a number of ways:

- Selecting an object to apply an editing technique to it (such as changing the brightness or contrast) without affecting the rest of the image

- Selecting a particular colour in an image

- Selecting an area to apply a special effect to it

- Selecting an area to remove it

Elements has several tools that can be used to select items and there are also a number of editing functions that can be applied to selections.

Two examples of how selections can be used are:

Once a selection has been made it stays selected even when another tool is activated, to allow for editing to take place.

Select an object and delete it

The best way to deselect a selection is to click on it once with one of the selection tools, preferably the one used to make the selection.

2 Select an area and add a colour or special effect

Marquee tools

There are two options for the Marquee tool: the Rectangular Marquee tool and the Elliptical Marquee tool. Both of these can be used to make symmetrical selections. To use the Marquee tools:

To access additional tools from the Toolbox, click and hold on the black triangle next to one of the default tools and select one of the subsequent options.

1 Select either the Rectangular or the Elliptical Marquee tool from the Toolbox and select the required options from the Options bar

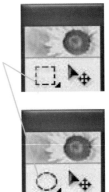

To make a selection that is exactly square or round, hold down Shift when dragging with the Rectangular Marquee tool or the Elliptical Marquee tool respectively.

2 Make a symmetrical selection with one of the tools by clicking and dragging on an image

Elliptical selection

Rectangular selection

Lasso tools

There are three options for the Lasso tools, which can be used to make freehand selections. To use these:

Lasso tool

1 Select the Lasso tool from the Toolbox and select the required options from the Options bar

When a selection has been completed (i.e. its end point reaches its start point), a small circle will appear at the side of whichever Lasso tool is being used. Click at this point to complete the selection.

2 Make a freehand selection by clicking and dragging around an object

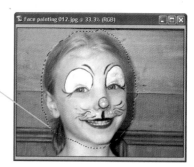

Polygonal Lasso tool

1 Select the Polygonal Lasso tool from the Toolbox and select the required options from the Options bar

Making a selection with the Polygonal Lasso tool is like creating a dot-to-dot pattern.

2 Make a selection by clicking on points around an object

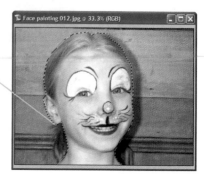

Magnetic Lasso tool

1 Select the Magnetic Lasso tool from the Toolbox and select the required options from the Options bar

On the Options bar for the Magnetic Lasso tool, the Edge Contrast value determines the amount of contrast there has to be between two colours for the selection line to snap to them. A high value detects lines with a high contrast and vice versa.

2 Click once to create the first anchor point

The Frequency setting on the Options bar determines how quickly the fastening points are inserted as a selection is being made. A high value places the fastening points more quickly than a low value.

3 Make a selection by dragging continuously around an object. The selection line automatically snaps to the closest strongest edge

i.e. the one with the most contrast. Fastening points are added as the selection is being made

Magic Wand tool

The Magic Wand tool can be used to select areas of the same, or similar, colour. To do this:

On the Options bar for the Magic Wand tool, the Tolerance box determines the range of colours that will be selected in relation to the colour you click on. A low value will only select a very narrow range of colours in relation to the initially selected one, while a high value will include a greater range.
The values range from 0–255.

1 Select the Magic Wand tool from the Toolbox and select the required options from the Options bar

2 Click on a colour to select all of the adjacent pixels that are the same, or similar, colour, depending on the options selected from the Options bar

On the Options bar for the Magic Wand tool, check on the Contiguous box to ensure that only adjacent colours are selected. To select the same, or similar, colour throughout the image, whether adjacent or not, check off the Contiguous box.

Colours outside the tolerance are not included within the selection

Selection Brush tool

The Selection Brush tool can be used to select areas by using a brush-like stroke. Unlike the Marquee or Lasso tools, the area selected by the Selection Brush tool is the one directly below where the tool moves. To make a selection with the Selection Brush tool:

1 Select the Selection Brush tool from the Toolbox and select the required options from the Options bar

The Selection Brush tool can be used to select an area or to mask an area. This can be determined in the Mode box in the Options bar.

2 Click and drag to make a selection

3 The selected area is underneath the borders of the Selection Brush tool

Inverting a selection

This can be a useful option if you have edited a selection and then you want to edit the rest of the image without affecting the area you have just selected. To do this:

1 Make a selection

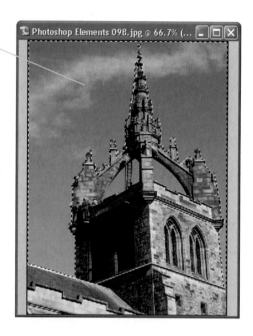

2 Choose Select>Inverse from the Menu bar

When inverting a selection, ensure that the whole of the required area has been selected. If not, hold down Shift and make another selection to add this to the existing one.

3 The selection becomes inverted i.e. if a background object was selected, the foreground is now selected

Feathering

Feathering is a technique that can be used to soften the edges of a selection by making them slightly blurry. This can be used if you are pasting a selection into another image or if you want to soften the edges around a portrait of an individual. To do this:

Feathering can also be selected from the Options bar once a Marquee tool is selected and before the selection has been made.

1 Make a selection

2 Choose Select> Feather from the Menu bar

Feathering can also be used to help achieve a depth of field effect, where part of the image is in focus (usually the foreground) and the rest is blurred.

To do this, make a selection and feather it. Then invert the selection and apply blurring (Filter>Blur>Gaussian Blur from the Menu bar). See Chapter Twelve for further details.

3 Enter a Feather value (the number of pixels around the radius of the selection that will be blurred). Click OK

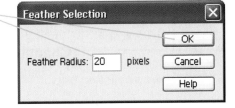

If required, crop the final image so that the feathered subject is more prominent.

4 Invert the selection as shown on the previous page and delete the background by pressing Delete (Windows) or Backspace (Mac). This will leave the subject with softened edges

Editing selections

When you've made a selection, you can edit it in a number of ways.

Moving
To move a selected area:

Once an area has been moved and deselected, it cannot then be selected independently again, unless it has been copied and pasted onto another layer.

1. Make a selection and select the Move tool from the Toolbox:

2. Drag the selection to move it to a new location

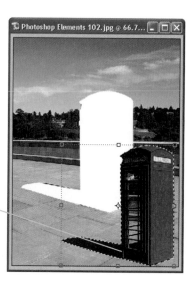

To deselect a selection, click once inside the selection area with the tool that was used to make the selection.

Changing the selection area
To change the area under the selection:

1. Make a selection with a selection tool

When changing the selection area, make sure that the New selection button is selected in the Options bar.

2. With the same tool selected, click and drag within the selection area to move it over another part of the image

Adding to a selection

To add to an existing selection:

1 Make a selection and click here in the Options bar:

Additions to selections can also be made by holding down Shift and making another selection.

2 Make another selection to create a single, larger, selection. The two selections do not have to interact

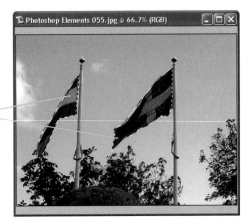

Subtractions can be made from a selection by selecting the 'Subtract from selection' button in the Options bar and then clicking and dragging from inside the selection.

Intersecting with a selection

To create a selection by intersecting two existing selections:

1 Make a selection and click here in the Options bar:

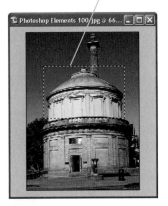

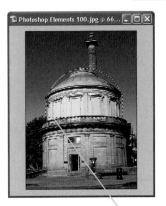

2 Make another selection that intersects the first. The intersected area will become the selection

Selections can be contracted in a similar way to expanding them, by selecting Select>Modify>Contract from the Menu bar. The amount for the selection to be contracted is then entered in the Contract Selection dialog box.

Expanding a selection

To expand a selection by a specific number of pixels:

1. Make a selection and choose Select>Modify>Expand from the Menu bar

2. In the Expand Selection dialog box, enter the amount by which you want the selection expanded. Click OK

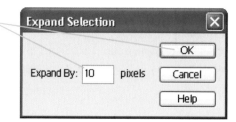

Growing a selection

The Grow command can be used on a selection when it has been made with the Magic Wand tool and some of the pixels within the selection have been omitted, due to being outside the tolerance. To do this:

1. Make a selection with the Magic Wand tool and choose Select>Grow from the Menu bar

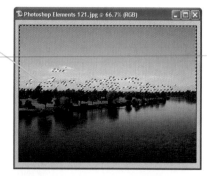

The Similar command (Select>Similar from the Menu bar) increases the selection in the same way as the Grow command, except that it includes non-adjacent pixels throughout the image.

2. Depending on the selections in the Options bar, the omitted pixels are included in the selection

Layers

For the artistically-minded who want to create more complex designs and effects with their images, the concept of layers is an invaluable one. It provides the means to add numerous elements to an image and edit them independently from one another. This chapter looks at how to use layers and also how they can be utilised to create fill effects and adjustment effects that can be applied without altering the original image.

Covers

Chapter Seven

Layering images

Layering is a technique that enables you to add additional elements to an image and place them on separate layers so that they can be edited and manipulated independently from other elements in the image. It is like creating an image using transparent sheets of film: each layer is independent of the others but, when they are combined, a composite image is created. This is an extremely versatile technique for working with digital images.

By using layers, several different elements can be combined to create a composite image:

Layers should usually be used when you are adding content to an image as this gives more flexibility for working with the various image elements.

Original image

Final image, with text and a shape added (two additional layers have been added)

Layers palette

The use of layers within Elements is governed by the Layers palette. When an image is first opened it is shown in the Layers palette as the Background layer. While this remains as the Background layer it cannot be moved above any other layers. However, it can be converted into a normal layer, in which case it operates in the same way as any other layers. To convert a Background layer into a normal one:

The Background layer can be converted into a normal one by applying certain editing functions to the image. These are the Background Eraser tool, the Magic Eraser tool and the Red Eye Brush tool.

1 The open image is shown here in the Layers palette as the Background

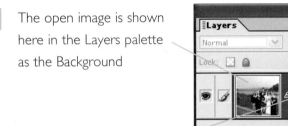

2 Double-click here

3 Enter a name for the layer and click OK

The Layers palette menu can be accessed by clicking on the More button in the Layers palette.

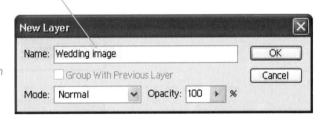

4 The layer becomes a normal layer in the Layers palette

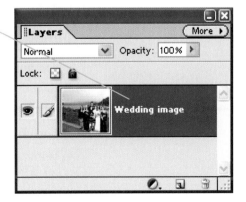

Adding layers

New blank layers can be added whenever you want to include new content within an image. This could be part of another image that has been copied and pasted, a whole new image, text or an object. To add a new layer:

Text is automatically added on a new layer and it is usually the topmost layer in an image.

1 Click here on the Layers palette

2 Double-click here and overtype to give the layer a specific name

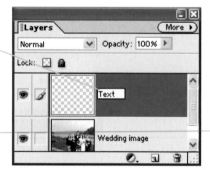

To edit an item on a particular layer, first make sure that the correct layer is selected in the Layers palette. A selected layer is known as the active layer and it is highlighted in the Layers palette with a solid colour through it.

3 With the new layer selected in the Layers palette, add content to the layer. This will be visible over the layer, or layers, below it

Fill layers

Fill layers can be added to images to give a gradient or solid colour effect behind or above the main subject. To do this:

1. With an image open, click here at the bottom right of the Layers palette

2. Select one of the fill options

3. For a Solid fill, select a colour from the Color Picker and click OK

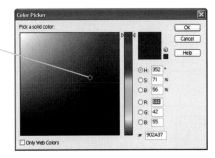

4. For a Gradient fill, click here to select a gradient style and click OK

5. For a Pattern fill, click here to select a pattern and click OK

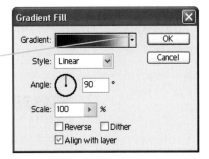

The Magic Eraser tool can also be used to create transparent areas in an image.

4 If the main image has a transparent background, the Fill layer will be visible behind it as long as the Fill layer is below the main image in the Layers palette. If not, click on it and drag it below the layer containing the main image

5 The Fill layer will cover anything below it, unless its opacity setting is changed in the Layers palette (see page 111 for details)

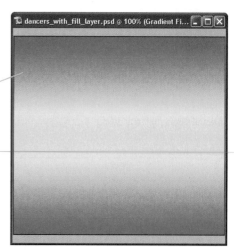

If you want to edit a Fill or Adjustment layer, double-click on its icon in the Layer palette and then apply the required changes. To change the type of layer, select Layer> Change Layer Content from the Menu bar and select the new attributes for the layer.

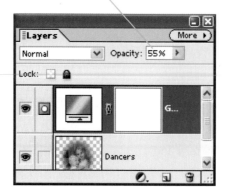

Adjustment layers

Adjustment layers can be used to apply common colour editing techniques, such as brightness and contrast, to an image without affecting the image itself, or any items above the Adjustment layer. The adjustment effect is added to a layer which allows the image below to be viewed through this layer. To do this:

Adjustment layers affect any visible content on all of the layers below them, not just the one immediately below.

1 With an image open, click here on the Layers palette

Although the Adjustment layer looks as if it has altered the image below it, it is in fact sitting above the image and has not affected it at all.

2 Select one of the adjustment options

3 Make editing changes for the selected adjustment item (in this example it is the Hue/ Saturation). Click OK

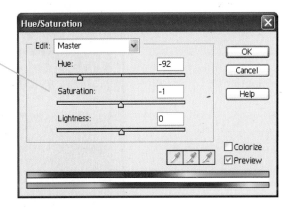

4 The effect in the Adjustment layer covers all of the layers below it. However, the layers themselves are untouched

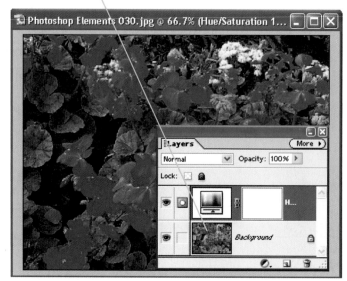

Both Fill and Adjustment layers are layer masks. This is a technique that enables the effect to be visible through the area of the mask.

5 If content is added on layers above the Adjustment layer, this will be unaffected by the settings in the Adjustment layer

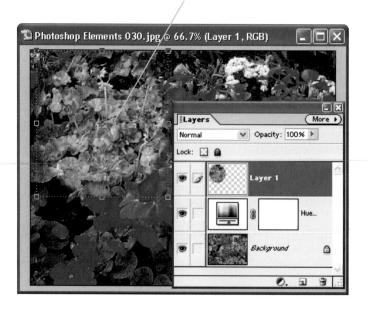

Working with layers

Moving layers

The order in which layers are arranged in the Layers palette is known as the stacking order. It is possible to change a layer's position in the stacking order, which affects how it is viewed in the composite image. To do this:

Click and drag a layer up or down to change its stacking order

Layers can be deleted by selecting them and clicking on the Wastebasket icon in the Layers palette. However, this also deletes all of the content on that layer.

Hiding layers

Layers can be hidden while you are working on other parts of an image. However, the layer is still part of the composite image, it has not been removed. To do this:

Click here so that the Eye icon disappears. Click again to reveal it

The tooltip that shows up for the Padlock icon is Lock All. This applies to all of the elements of the selected layer, not all of the layers within the Layers palette.

Locking layers

Layers can be locked so that they cannot accidentally be edited while you are working on other parts of an image. To do this:

Click here so that a padlock appears next to the selected layer

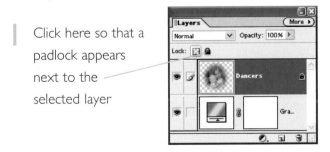

Blending layers

Blending is a technique that enables two layers to interact with each other in a variety of ways. To do this:

1 Select a layer either in the Layers palette or by clicking on the relevant item within an image

There are over twenty blend options. Experiment with them to see what effects they create.

2 Click here on the Layers palette

3 Select an option from the Blend menu

4 The selected blend option determines how the selected layer interacts with the one below it

Opacity

The opacity of a layer can be set to determine how much of the layer below is visible through the selected layer. To do this:

1 Select a layer either in the Layers palette or by clicking on the relevant item within an image

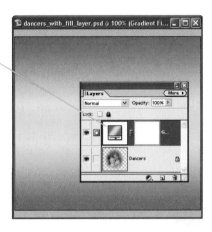

Opacity is a good technique for creating a watermark effect. To do this, create a layer above the Background layer and set it to an opacity of approximately 20%–30%.

2 Enter the opacity level here. The greater the amount of opacity, the less transparent the selected layer becomes

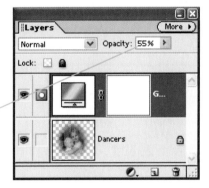

3 The opacity setting determines how much of the layer below is visible through the selected one

Saving layers

Once an image has been created using two or more layers there are two ways in which the composite image can be saved: in a proprietary Photoshop format, in which case individual layers are maintained, or in a general file format, in which case all of the layers will be merged into a single one. The advantage of the former is that individual elements can still be edited within the image, independently of other items. In general, it is good practise to save layered images in both a Photoshop and a non-Photoshop format. To save layered images in a Photoshop format:

1   Select File>Save As from the Menu bar

HOT TIP

Before a layer is saved it is possible to create a composite image consisting of a single layer. To do this, select Layer>Flatten Image from the Menu bar. To merge the existing layer and the one below it, select Layer>Merge Down from the Menu bar and to merge all visible content (excluding any layers that have been hidden) select Layer> Merge Visible.

2   Make sure Photoshop (*.PSD, *.PDD) is selected as the format

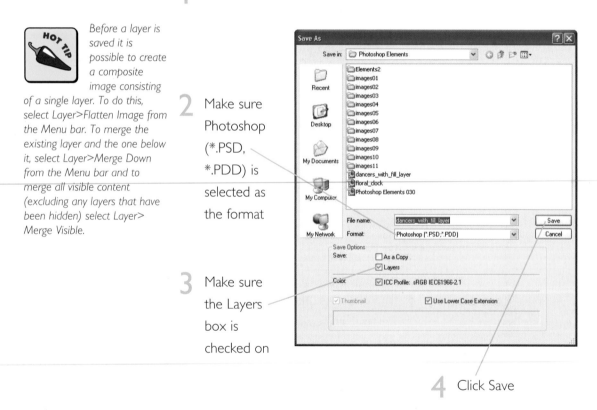

3   Make sure the Layers box is checked on

4   Click Save

To save in a non-Photoshop format, select File>Save As from the Menu bar. Select a file format from the Format box and click OK. The Layers box will not be available.

Text and drawing objects

Elements offers a lot more than just the ability to edit digital images. It also has options for adding and formatting text and creating a variety of graphical objects. This chapter looks at how to add these items and also edit them using the drawing tools that are available.

Covers

Chapter Eight

Adding and formatting text

Text can be added to images in Elements and this can be used to create a wide range of items such as cards, brochures and posters. To add text to an image:

1 Select the Horizontal or Vertical Type tool from the Menu bar:

2 Click once on the image with the Type tool

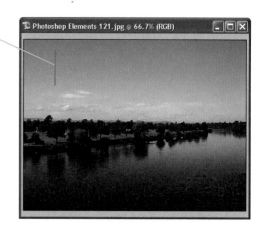

3 Make the required formatting selections from the Options bar:

Font style   Font type   Font size   Anti-aliased

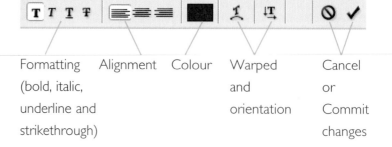

Formatting   Alignment   Colour   Warped   Cancel
(bold, italic,   and   or
underline and   orientation   Commit
strikethrough)   changes

4 Type the text onto the image. This is automatically placed on a new layer at the top of the stacking order in the Layers palette

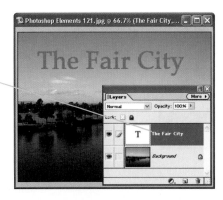

5 To move the text, select it with the Move tool and click and drag it to a new position

Further formatting effects can be applied to text through the use of Layer Styles. For more information about this, see page 121.

To format text that has already been entered:

1 Select a Type tool and drag it over a piece of text to select it

2 Make the changes in the Options bar as shown in Step 3 on the facing page

Distorting text

In addition to producing standard text, it is also possible to create some dramatic effects by distorting text. To do this:

1 Enter plain text and select it by dragging a Type tool over it

2 Click Create Warped Text in the Options bar:

3 Click here and select one of the options in the Warp Text dialog box. Click OK

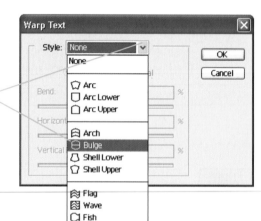

4 The selected effect is applied to the text

Text masks

Text masks can be used to reveal an area of an image showing through the text. This can be used to produce eye-catching headings and slogans. To do this:

1 Select the Horizontal or the Vertical Type Mask tool from the Toolbox:

2 Click on an image and enter and format text as you would for normal text. A red mask is applied to the image when the mask text is entered

HOT TIP *Text mask effects work best if the text used is fairly large in size. In some cases it is a good idea to use bold text, as this is wider than standard text.*

3 Press Enter or click on the Move tool to border the mask text with dots

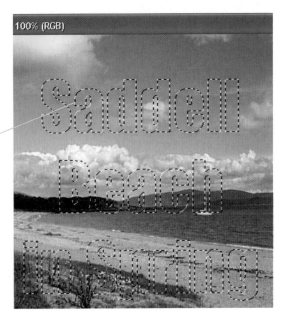

4 Select Edit>Copy from the Menu bar

5 Select File>New from the Menu bar

Once a text mask has been copied it can also be pasted into other types of documents such as Word and desktop publishing documents.

6 The size of the new file matches that of the copied text mask. Click OK

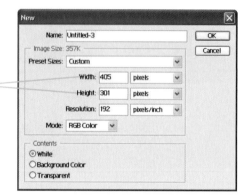

7 Select Edit>Paste from the Menu bar

8 The text appears with the original image behind it

Adding shapes

Another way to add extra style to your images is through the use of shapes. There are several types of symmetrical shapes that can be added to images and also a range of custom ones. To add shapes to an image:

1 Click and hold on the Rectangle tool in the Toolbox

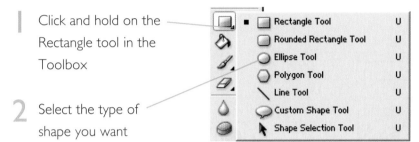

Rectangle Tool	U
Rounded Rectangle Tool	U
Ellipse Tool	U
Polygon Tool	U
Line Tool	U
Custom Shape Tool	U
Shape Selection Tool	U

The tools for creating shapes are also available from the Options bar when the Rectangle tool (or any related tools) is selected.

2 Select the type of shape you want

3 Click and drag on the image to create the required shape

4 If you want to change the colour of a shape, click here in the Options bar and select a new colour. This can be done either before the shape is created or it can be used to edit the colour of an existing shape, when selected with the Move tool

Color:

Custom shapes

Custom shapes can be used to add pre-designed graphical objects rather than just symmetrical shapes. To do this:

1   Select the Custom Shape tool from the Toolbox or from the Options bar

Each new shape is added on a new layer. However, shapes on two different layers can be linked by clicking on the box to the right of the Eye icon in the Layers palette. They can then be moved, rotated or transformed together even though they remain on different layers. Items in different layers can also be linked by Shift+clicking on them.

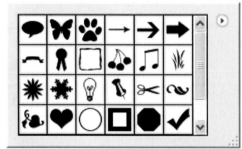

2   Click here in the Options bar to view custom shapes. Click on one to select it

3   Click and drag to add a custom shape to an image

Layer Styles

When plain text and objects are added to images, they appear as two-dimensional items. If you want to give them a 3-D effect, this can be achieved through the use of the Layer Styles palette.

To do this:

Layer Styles can be applied to symmetrical objects and also custom ones.

1 Drag the Layer Styles palette from the palette well

2 Click here to select the available styles

The Drop Shadow styles are a good option for adding emphasis to textual items such as headings. However, as with most effects, don't overuse them.

3 Select an object or a piece of text with the Move tool and click once on a style in the Layers Style palette to apply that style to the selected item in the image

Paint Bucket tool

The Paint Bucket tool can be used to add a solid colour to a selection or an object. To do this:

1 Select an area within an image or select an object

Use the Move tool to select objects or text.

2 Select the Paint Bucket tool from the Toolbox:

For more information on working with colour, see pages 127–128.

3 Click here in the Toolbox to access the Color Picker for changing the currently selected colour

4 Click once on the selected area or object to change its colour to the one loaded in the Paint Bucket tool

Gradient tool

The Gradient tool can be used to add a gradient fill to a selection or an object. To do this:

If no selection is made for a gradient fill, the effect will be applied to the entire selected layer.

1   Select an area in an image or select an object

2   Select the Gradient tool from the Toolbox:

3   Click here in the Options bar to select preset gradient fills

The default gradient in the Options bar is created with the current foreground and background Toolbox colours.

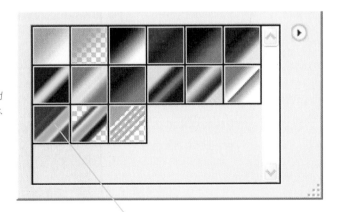

4   Click on a gradient style to apply it as the default

5 Click here in the Options bar to access the Gradient Editor dialog

To create a new preset gradient, create it in the Gradient Editor dialog box and click on the New button to add it to the list of preset gradients. Double-click on the gradient's icon to give it a name in the Gradient Name dialog box.

6 Click and drag the sliders to change the amount of a particular colour in the gradient

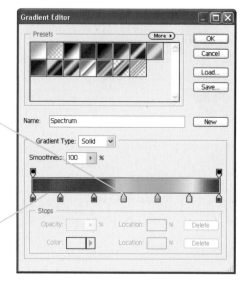

7 Click along here to add a new colour marker. Click OK

The amount that the cursor is dragged when adding a gradient determines where the centrepoint of the gradient is located and also the size of each segment of the gradient.

8 Click an icon in the Options bar to select a gradient style:

9 Click and drag within the selection or object to specify the start and end point of the gradient effect

Brush and Pencil tools

The Brush and Pencil tools work in a similar way and can be used to create lines of varying thickness and style. To do this:

1 Select the Brush tool or Pencil tool from the Toolbox:

The Mode options for the Brush and Pencil tools are similar to those for blending layers together. They include options such as Darken, Lighten, Soft Light and Difference. Each of these enables the line to blend with the image below it.

2 Select the required options from the Options bar

3 Click and drag to create lines on an image

The Brush and Pencil tools are very similar in the way they function, except that the Brush tool has more options and can create more subtle effects.

Impressionist Brush tool

The Impressionist Brush tool can be used to create a dappled effect over an image, similar to an impressionist painting. To do this:

1. Select the Impressionist Brush tool from the Toolbox:

If the Impressionist Brush tool is not visible in the Toolbox, click and hold on the black triangle next to the Brush tool and select it from the menu.

2. Select the required options from the Options bar

3. Click and drag over an image to create an impressionist effect

If the brush size is too large for the Impressionist Brush tool, it can result in the effect being too extreme and a lot of an image's definition being lost.

Working with colour

All of the text and drawing tools make extensive use of colour. Elements provides a number of methods for selecting colours and also for working with them.

Foreground and background colours

At the bottom of the Toolbox there are two coloured squares. These represent the currently selected foreground and background colours. The foreground colour, which is the most frequently used, is the one that is applied to drawing objects, such as fills and lines, and also text. The background colour is used for items such as as gradient fills and for areas that have been removed with the Eraser tool.

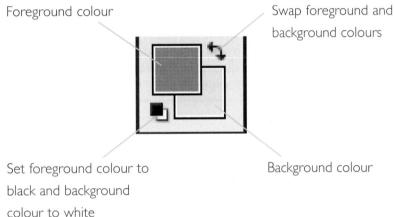

Foreground colour

Swap foreground and background colours

Set foreground colour to black and background colour to white

Background colour

Whenever the foreground or background colour squares are clicked on, the Eyedropper tool is automatically activated. This can be used to select a colour, from anywhere on your screen, in addition to using the Color Picker.

Color Picker

The Color Picker can be used to select a new colour for the foreground or background colour. To do this:

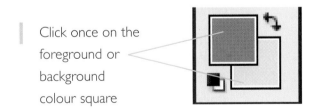

Click once on the foreground or background colour square

2 In the Color Picker click to select a colour

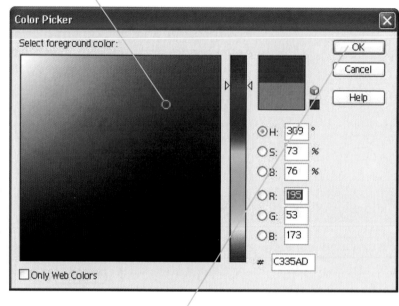

3 Click OK

Swatches palette

The Swatches palette can be used to access different colour palettes that can then be used as the foreground and background colours. To do this:

1 Drag the Swatches palette from the palette well

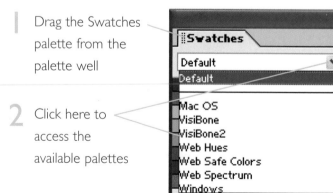

2 Click here to access the available palettes

Effects and filters

One of the most exciting aspects of digital imaging is the ability to creating stunning special effects. This chapter looks at some of the effects that can be used in Elements and shows you how to apply them.

Covers

Chapter Nine

Applying effects

Applying effects is one of the most satisfying parts of digital image editing: it is quick and the results can be dramatic. Effects can be applied to entire images, or to a selected area. Effects are created using the Effects palette. To apply effects:

1 Open an image or select part of an image

 To display the items in the Effects palette as a list, click the List View button at the bottom right of the palette.

2 Drag the Effects palette from the palette well

3 Click here to access available categories and choose one

4 Double-click on an effect or click on it once and click Apply for it to take effect on the image or selection

Examples of effects

Colorful Center

You can apply effects to images and also selected text in images.

If you do not like a particular effect, click on the Step Backward button on the Shortcuts bar after it has been applied.

Fluorescent Chalk

Rubber Stamp

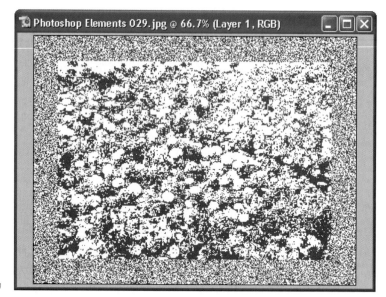

Wild Frame

Brushed Metal (Type)

In the examples on this page, the type has been placed on a coloured rectangle to enable it to stand out from the background.

Type effects can only be applied if there is a Type layer on the page i.e. type has already been added to the image. Some effects can only be applied to type.

Confetti (Type)

Green Slime (Background)

The background effects can be applied to new, blank files, as a base onto which other elements can be placed.

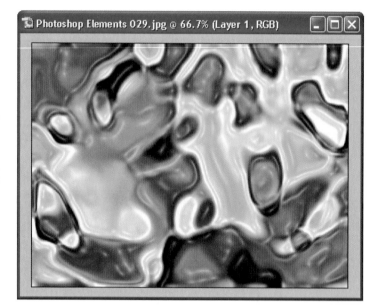

Sunset (Background)

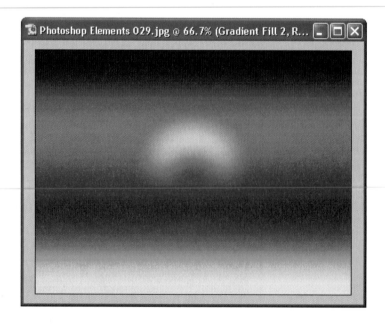

Applying filters

Filters can be used to create similar results to effects; however, for most filters there is an additional dialog so you can edit their attributes. Filters can be used on entire images or selected areas.

To use filters:

The available filters can also be accessed from the Filter menu on the Menu bar.

1 Open an image or select part of an image

2 Drag the Filters palette from the palette well

3 Click here to access available categories and choose one

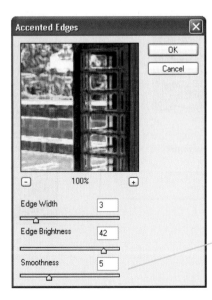

4 Double-click on a filter or click on it once and click Apply to access the filter's dialog box

5 Make the required selections in the dialog box and click OK

Examples of filters

Add Noise

Dialog box

Effect

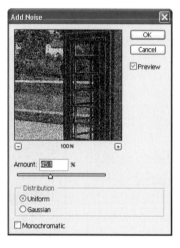

In general, it is not a good idea to add a filter to an image that has already had one applied to it. This just serves to lessen the impact of both of the filters used.

Bas Relief

Dialog box

Effect

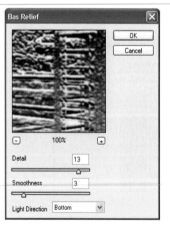

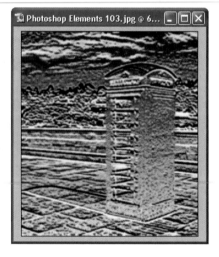

Lens Flare

Dialog box

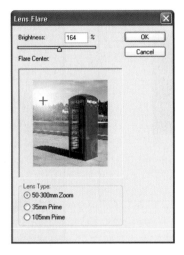

Effect

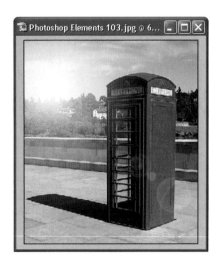

Motion Blur can be added to a background behind a vehicle or a person to create the impression of speed. For more information about this, see Chapter Twelve.

Motion Blur

Dialog box

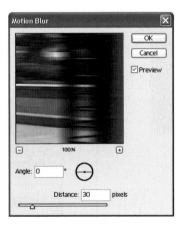

Effect

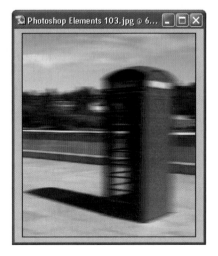

Ripple

Dialog box   **Effect**

 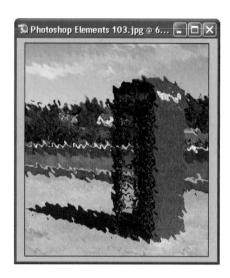

Wind

Dialog box   **Effect**

 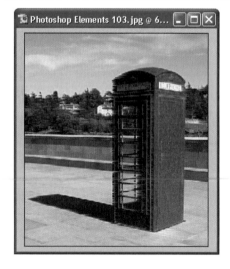

Liquify filter

The Liquify filter is an option that can be accessed by selecting Filter>Distort>Liquify from the Menu bar or from the Liquify option on the Filters palette. It has its own window from which various options can be selected for different liquify effects. The purpose of the Liquify filter is to enable you to create effects by dragging different tools across the surface of an image and rearranging the pixels accordingly.

To use the Liquify filter:

1 Select Filter>Distort>Liquify from the Menu bar or select the Liquify option on the Filters palette

The tools in the Liquify filter are (from top to bottom): Warp, Turbulence, Twirl Clockwise, Twirl Counter Clockwise, Pucker, Bloat, Shift Pixels, Reflection, Reconstruct, Zoom and Hand.

2 Select a tool

3 Select tool options

4 Drag the tool across the surface of the image

5 Click OK

Creating liquify effects

Creating a reflection

To create a reflection of an image:

1   Select the Reflection tool:

2   Drag the Reflection tool from right to left under the area of the image that you want to reflect

If you want to reflect an area from below the Reflection tool, drag it from left to right.

3   Select the Warp tool

4   Drag the Warp tool diagonally across the reflected part of the image to give it a more rippled effect

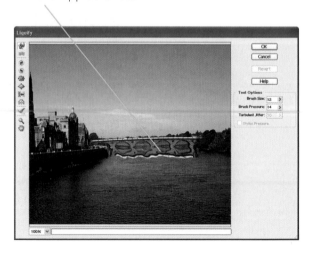

Warping, puckering and bloating

These tools can be used, among other things, to change facial expressions:

1 The original image

2 Select the Warp tool and drag to achieve facial distortions

3 Select the Pucker tool and drag to decrease the size of image areas

4 Select the Bloat tool and drag it to increase the size of areas of the image

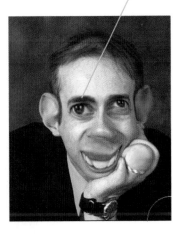

Creating fire and waves

The Turbulence tool can be used to create fire and wave effects with images and also text:

1 Select the Turbulence tool

If you are using one of the Liquify tools on text, the text layer has to first be simplified. This can be done by selecting the text layer and selecting Layer>Simplify Layer from the Menu bar.

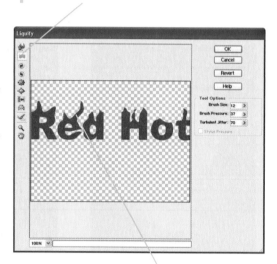

2 Drag it over text to create a fire effect

3 Drag it over water to create a wave effect

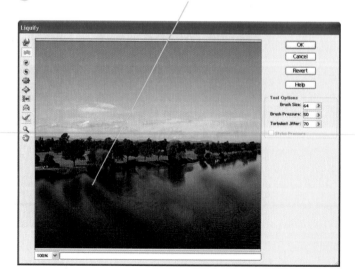

Images for the Web

It is increasingly common for photographic images to be used on Web pages and as attachments to emails. However, in a lot of cases problems occur because the files that are used are too large and take too long to download.

This chapter looks at some of the issues concerning images that are being used on the Web or with emails. This includes suitable file formats and the process of optimisation. It also looks at creating an online gallery of photographs and shows how to create animated effects for the Web.

Covers

Chapter Ten

File formats for the Web

Digital images can be created and saved in a variety of different formats. This is not always immediately apparent when you view the images on screen, but the file format can have important implications as far as the use of the image is concerned.

The main areas that designers of image file formats consider are:

- The size of files – how to get good quality images that do not take up a lot of disc space

- The quality of images – how to produce images that give the best published quality possible

For these reasons, particular file formats are used for images on Web pages.

GIF files

GIF (Graphical Interchange Format) is one of the two main file formats that are used for images on the Web (the other being JPEG). It was designed with this specifically in mind and its main advantage is that it creates image files that are relatively small. It achieves this principally by compressing the image by removing unnecessary or irrelevant data in the file.

The main drawback with GIF files for digital images is that they can only display a maximum of 256 colours. This is considerably less than the 16 million colours that can be used in a full colour image. Therefore photographs in a GIF format may lose some colour definition and they will not have the same range of colour subtleties as a format that can display the full range of colours.

Despite its narrow colour range GIF is still a very useful and popular format. It is excellent for displaying graphics and even photographs can be of a perfectly acceptable standard for display on the Web. Add to this the fact that it can create very small image files and it is easy to see why GIF is so popular with Web designers and graphic artists who work in this area.

GIFs use lossless compression to achieve smaller file sizes.

JPEG files

JPEG (Joint Photographic Experts Group) is the other main file format for Web images and it is the one that, as the name suggests, specialises in photographic images. Most digital cameras automatically save images as JPEGs.

JPEG images only achieve their full effect on the Web if the user's monitor is set to 16 million colours (also known as 24 bit). Most modern monitors are capable of doing this but, in some cases, the user may have set the monitor to a lower specification.

If you are concerned about how your images are going to be viewed, it may be worth putting a note on your site suggesting that the screen be set to 16 million colours for full effect.

As with GIF, JPEG compresses the image so that the file size is smaller; it is therefore quicker to download on the Web. One downside to this is that the file is compressed each time it is opened and saved, so the image quality deteriorates correspondingly. When a file is opened, it is automatically decompressed but if this is done numerous times then it can result in an inferior image.

The main advantage of JPEG files is that they can display over 16 million colours. This makes them ideal for displaying photographic images. The colour quality of the image is retained and the file size is still suitably small.

JPEGs use lossy compression for smaller file sizes.

PNG files

The PNG (Portable Network Group) file format is a relatively new one in the Web image display market but it is becoming more popular with designers. It uses 16 million colours and lossless compression, as opposed to JPEG which uses lossy compression. The result is better image quality but a slightly larger file size. Since PNG is a less common format there are a few factors to bear in mind when using it:

Gif files have a .gif extension, JPEG files .jpeg or .jpg and PNG files .png.

- Not all browsers support the PNG format. This will undoubtedly change as its use becomes more widespread but it is a consideration at the moment

- PCs and Macs use different PNG file types and, although both types can be opened and viewed on both platforms, they appear to their best effect on the platforms on which they were created

- PNG files can contain meta-tags – indexing information that can be read by Web search engines when someone is looking for your website

Saving images for the Web

The most crucial issue for images that are going to be used on the Web is file size. This must be small enough so that the images can be downloaded quickly on a Web page, otherwise the user will become impatient and move onto another site. To assist in this, Elements has a function for saving images in different formats and also altering the quality settings for each format. This enables you to balance the image quality and file size so that you have the optimum image for use on the Web. To do this:

Try to keep images that are going to be used on the Web well under 100K in file size. If possible, a file size in the region of 30–50K is desirable.

1 Open an image and select File>Save for Web from the Menu bar

2 The original image is shown here

Preparing images for the Web is also known as optimising them.

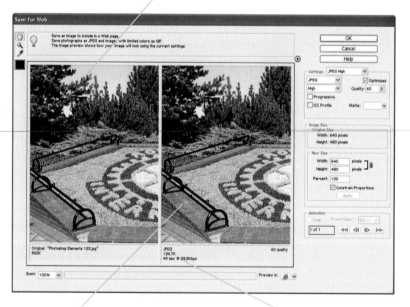

3 The preview of the optimised image is shown here. This is how the image will look in the selected file format and also with the quality settings that have been specified

4 The new file size and download time at a specified modem speed display here

...cont'd

5 Click here to select a file format

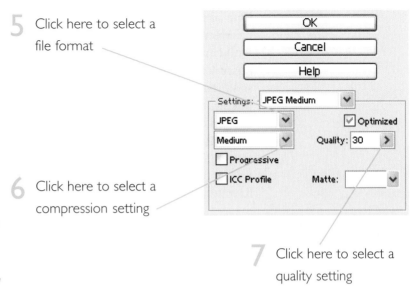

6 Click here to select a compression setting

7 Click here to select a quality setting

8 Click OK to activate the Save Optimized As window. A copy of the original image can be saved here. A new image is created, based on the original name but with hyphens inserted. Click Save

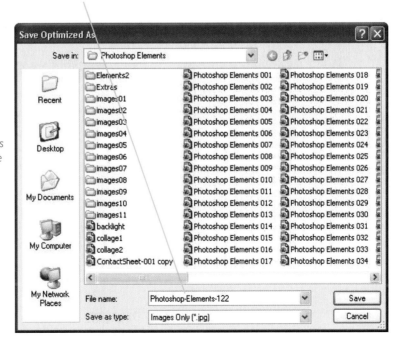

Emailing images

One of the most common ways of transferring images electronically is by email. However, the same rules apply here as with images on the Web – the file size should be as small as possible. A good way to alienate friends and work colleagues is to send them large attachments as part of an email. It is not uncommon for people to send images over 1Mb in size, which can take several minutes to download. Elements takes this into account when attaching images to emails, but it is also worth optimising them yourself before you attach them to an email. Rather than having to open your email program separately, Elements has a function for attaching images directly to an email:

If changes have been made to the image and they have not been saved, a dialog will appear asking you to save the image before it is emailed. Click Save As and Continue and then save the image before it is attached to an email.

1 Open an image and, in the Menu bar, select File>Attach to E-mail

2 If the image is not a JPEG click Auto Convert in the Attach to E-mail dialog box (Windows only)

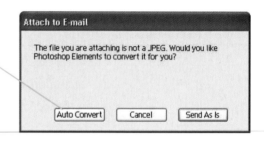

The Attach to E-mail command automatically compresses the image to make it quicker to send over the Internet.

3 The default email program is opened with the image attached. Complete the email and click Send

Creating a Web Photo Gallery

Displaying photographs on the Web is a popular way to share them with family and friends. If you are a budding Web author, you can do this by creating the Web pages (in HTML) and then inserting the required images. However, Elements simplifies the process and removes the need to know anything about the inner workings of Web authoring and design. Instead, the Web Photo Gallery creates Web pages with the required images already inserted.

To use the Web Photo Gallery:

HTML stands for HyperText Markup Language and it is the code that is used to create pages for the Web. For more information about this, see 'HTML in easy steps'.

1 Select File>Create Web Photo Gallery from the Menu bar

2 Click here to select a style for the Web Photo Gallery

3 Enter an email address for the Gallery

When creating a Web Photo Gallery, create a sub-folder into which the files for the Gallery will be placed.

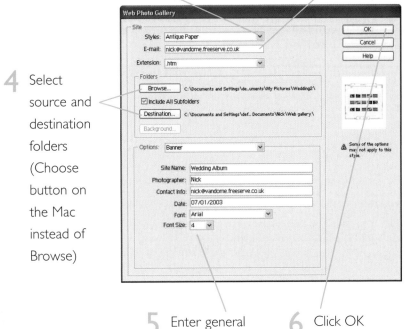

4 Select source and destination folders (Choose button on the Mac instead of Browse)

Leave the option under Extension as .htm which is the file extension that will be used for the HTML pages that are created. Although the extension .html can also be used, .htm is more common.

5 Enter general information here

6 Click OK

7 The Photo Gallery will be created and displayed in your browser

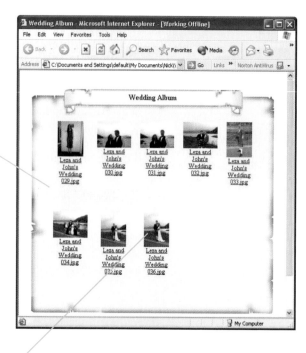

For more information about creating and publishing Web pages, have a look at 'Creating Web Pages in easy steps' in this series.

8 Click on a thumbnail to display the larger version of an image

9 Click here to move through the images in the Photo Gallery

Publishing a Web Photo Gallery

Once a Web Photo Gallery has been created it can then be displayed on the Web. This allows other people to view your photographs and creative work. To do this you will have to obtain a Web address (URL) and Web space from a Web hosting service. To publish your Photo Gallery:

URL stands for Uniform Resource Locator and it is a unique address for a Web page.

1 Locate the folder in which all of the Photo Gallery files have been created. This will include image files and HTML files

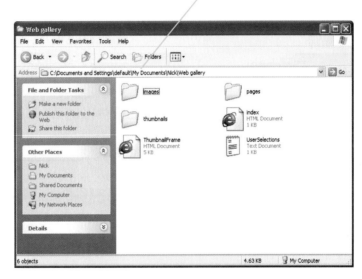

There are a number of sites on the Web that offer free Web hosting. These include: Yahoo GeoCities at http://uk.geocities.yahoo.com/ and AOL at http://www.aol.com.

2 Contact a Web hosting service, who will provide you with a Web address, Web space for your site and also details of how to publish your files:

3 Obtain a FTP (File Transfer Protocol) program. This will be used to transfer your Photo Gallery files from your own computer onto the one used by your Web hosting service

FTP programs can be downloaded from the Web and a lot of them are free.
Three to look at are:

- *www.ipswitch.com for WS_FTP*
- *www.bpftp.com for BulletProofFTP*
- *http://fetchsoftworks.com for Fetch (Mac users only)*

4 Once the files have been uploaded, they can be viewed on your own website, which can be accessed by anyone who has the Web address (URL)

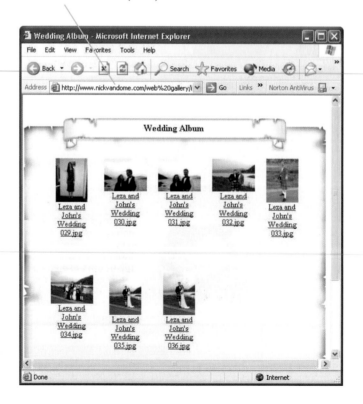

Creating Web buttons

For anyone interested in creating websites, graphical buttons are an integral part of the process: they serve as links to other pages and navigation bars. In Elements it is possible to create a wide range of buttons for use on Web pages. To do this:

1 Select File>New from the Menu bar and enter the dimensions for the size of button you want to create. Click OK

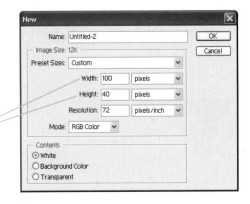

For more information on using the Layers Style palette, see Chapter Eight, page 121.

2 Select a Shape tool from the Toolbox

3 Draw a shape on the canvas

Once a Web button has been created, save it as a PSD file and a GIF file. Use the PSD file to create more buttons by copying it using Save As and changing the text on the text layer. Save each button as a GIF and use these on a Web page.

4 Apply a style from the Layers Style palette

5 Add text and, if desired, format it using the Layers Style palette

Creating PDF files

PDF (Portable Document Format) is a file format that is used to maintain the original formatting and style of a document so that it can be viewed on a variety of different devices and types of computers. In general, it is usually used for documents that contain text and images such as information pamphlets, magazine features and chapters from books. However, image files such as JPEGs can also be converted into PDF and this can be done within Elements without the need for any other special software. To do this:

The PDF format was developed by Adobe, so all PDF files created in Elements are certain to be compatible.

1 Click the Save as PDF button in the Shortcuts bar or select File>Save As from the Menu bar:

2 Select a destination folder for the file and make sure the file type is set to Photoshop PDF. Click Save

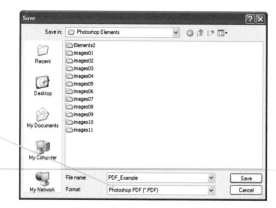

Unless you have Elements, the Adobe Acrobat Reader (downloadable free from www.adobe.com) has to be installed on a computer on which you want to view PDF files.

3 The PDF file can then be opened in Acrobat Reader or Elements

Creating Web animations

As well as displaying static images, Elements can also be used to create animated effects for use on the Web. Animations are created with the GIF file format and the effect is achieved by placing different objects on separate layers and then viewing the image so that each layer is displayed sequentially.

When creating a Web animation, work out the effect you want to achieve and then capture the images that will be used to create this effect.

To create an animation for use on the Web:

1 Open a blank image (File>New from the Menu bar) and drag the Layers palette from the palette well

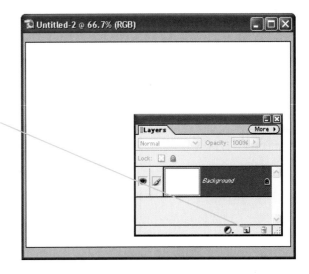

2 Add extra layers by clicking here

Animated images for use on the Web are usually larger in file size than static ones.

Items that are added to additional layers can included parts of the same image, or other images, that have been copied and pasted, or graphical elements that have been created using the tools in the Toolbox.

3 Add new content to each layer

4 Click on the Save for Web button in the Shortcuts bar or select File>Save for Web from the Menu bar

5 Select GIF as the file format and check on the Animate box

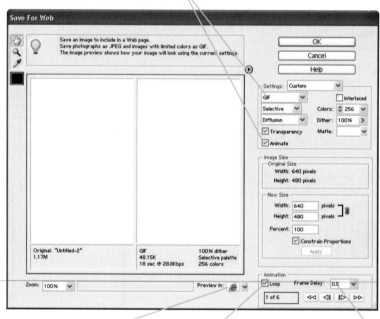

8 Click here to preview the animation in your default browser

7 Check on the Loop box if you want the animation to keep playing continuously

6 Enter a value for the time each layer is visible (1 = 1 second)

9 Click OK and save the image

Printing images

Printing digital images is one of their most common uses and the quality is now comparable with traditional film photographs. This chapter looks at general printing issues, how to size images for printing and how to select the best layout format for your printed output.

Covers

Chapter Eleven

Printing issues

Three of the top inkjet printer manufacturers are Epson, Canon and Hewlett Packard. Their websites can be found at (respectively):

- www.epson.co.uk
- www.canon.co.uk
- www.hp.co.uk

Printers

One of the biggest advances in the digital imaging process in recent years has been in the quality of the images when they are printed. Printers can now produce images that are virtually the same quality as images processed from traditional film cameras. There are three main types of printer that can be used to print digital images:

- Inkjet printers. These are the cheapest and the most common. In addition, they also produce excellent results. They work by placing tiny dots of colour on the paper to make up the image

- Laser printers. Colour laser printers are expensive and they are generally only a viable option in the workplace

- Dye-sublimation and thermal wax printers. Unlike inkjet printers, these printers place a continuous coating of ink on the paper rather than a series of dots. They produce excellent results but are more expensive than inkjet printers and do not have the same versatility in terms of paper size

The CMYK colour model is used to create printed images since printers cannot produce the exact same colours as the eye sees, which is the RGB (Red, Green, Blue) colour model. In CMYK Black is denoted by K rather than B so as not to confuse it with Blue.

Ink

When looking at printers, the question of ink is also an important one. Inkjet printers use a minimum of four colour cartridges (Cyan, Magenta, Yellow and Black, which produces the CMYK colour model). Some printers also have an extra two cartridges, which are usually variations of Cyan and Magenta, which produce more subtle skin tones. When looking at printers, check the cost of replacement cartridges as this could be an important factor in the overall running costs of the printer.

Some companies sell non-branded ink cartridges. While these are cheaper than the branded versions, the quality is not always as high.

Paper

There is a huge variety of paper available for printing digital images. If you want to get the very best results:

- Buy the same make of paper as your printer. This may be more expensive than other brands but it will be the most compatible with your printer and its printing technology

- Use the heaviest photo quality paper available

Print size

Before you start printing images in Elements it is important to ensure that they are going to be produced at the required size. Since the pixels within an image are not a set size, the printed dimensions of an image can be altered according to your needs. This is done by specifying how many pixels are used within each inch of the image. The more pixels per inch (ppi) then the higher the quality of the printed image, but the smaller in size it will be.

To set the print size of an image:

The higher the resolution in the Document Size section of the dialog, the greater the quality but the smaller the size of the printed image.

1 Open an image and select Image>Resize>Image Size from the Menu bar

2 Check off the Resample Image box. This will ensure that the physical image size i.e. the number of pixels in the image, remains unchanged when the resolution is changed

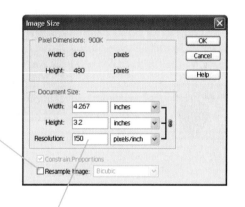

The output size for a printed image can be worked out by dividing the pixel dimensions (the width and height) by the resolution. So if the width is 1280, the height 960 and the resolution 300, the printed image will be roughly 4 inches by 3 inches.

3 The current resolution and document size (print size) are displayed here

4 Enter a new figure in the Resolution box (here the resolution has been reduced from 150 to 72). This affects the Document Size, the size at which the image prints

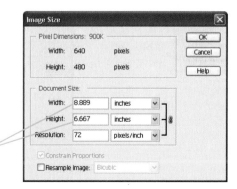

...cont'd

An image of 1280 x 960 pixels, set to print
at 150 pixels per inch (not actual size)

To achieve the best results, print images at a resolution of 150 ppi or above and set your printer to its highest dots per inch (dpi) setting. On current inkjet printers this is in the range of up to 5760 dpi.

Leza and John's Wedding 043.jpg @ 48% (RGB)

Dots per inch (dpi) and pixels per inch (ppi) are not the same. The term 'dots per inch' refers to the coloured dots produced by the printer and 'pixels per inch' refers to the number of coloured dots within an inch of the image itself.

An image of 1280 x 960 pixels set to print
at 300 pixels per inch (not actual size)

Leza and John's Wedding 043.jpg @ 24% (RGB)

As long as the Resample box is checked off, changing the output resolution has no effect on the actual number of pixels in an image.

Print Preview

The Print Preview function can be used to view how an image will look when it is printed. This can be a useful option for ensuring you do not waste too much paper when printing images.

To use Print Preview:

1 Click the Print Preview button in the Shortcuts bar or select File>Print Preview from the Menu bar

HOT TIP
To preview the print size of an image without accessing Print Preview, select the Zoom tool from the Toolbox and click the Print Size button in the Options bar.

2 Check on the Center Image box to centre the image on the paper when it is printed

3 Check off the Center Image box and drag the image elsewhere. Or specify a location from the top/left of the paper

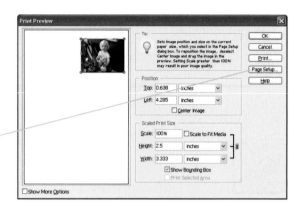

4 Click here to access the Page Setup dialog box

If you scale an image to print at greater than 100% there will be some deterioration in image quality. This is because the print size will be achieved by stretching each pixel to cover a greater area, which decreases the sharpness of the image.

5 Enter any required settings such as the page orientation (Portrait prints vertically, Landscape horizontally). Click OK

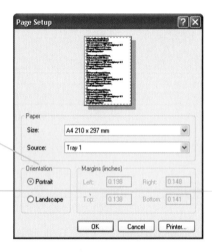

If you change the size at which an image is printed by entering a new value in the Scale box, this does not alter the resolution setting in the Image Size dialog box.

6 Enter a percentage value if you want the image to be printed at a smaller or larger size

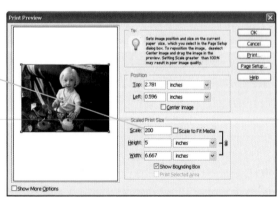

7 Click OK to keep the settings or Print to print the image

Print Layouts

Rather than just offering the sole function of printing a single image on a sheet of paper, Elements has two options that can be used when printing images, which can help conserve the number of sheets of paper used.

Contact Sheets

This can be used to create and print thumbnail versions of a large number of images. To do this:

1 Select File>Print Layouts>Contact Sheet from the Menu bar

When a contact sheet is created, new thumbnail images are generated. The original images are unaffected.

2 Click here (Choose on the Mac) to select a folder for the new contact sheet

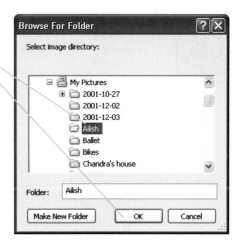

3 Select a folder and click OK

4 Enter details for the final output document, the size of the thumbnails in it and any caption to accompany the images

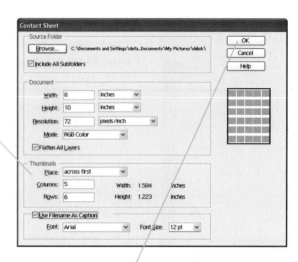

5 Click OK

The thumbnails within a contact sheet are created as a single image in the contact sheet file, rather than a series of individual images.

6 The contact sheet is created as a new file and can be printed like an individual image, using the File>Print command. If it is larger than the paper size, a dialog will appear asking if you want to scale the image to fit. Check on the Scale to Fit Media box and click OK

Contact sheet files are saved in the same way as individual images.

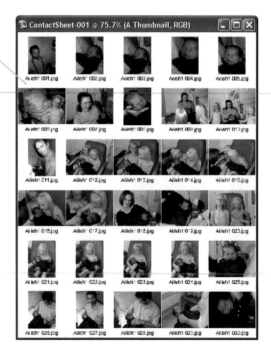

Picture Package

This can be used to print out multiple copies of the same image on a single piece of paper. To do this:

1. Select File>Print Layouts>Picture Package from the Menu bar

2. Click here to select a source for the image for the Picture Package. If File or Folder are selected, click on the Browse button (Choose button on the Mac) to select an individual file or folder

If Folder is selected for the source of the Picture Package, all of the images in the folder will be created as individual Picture Package files.

For the caption option to be available, select Custom Text in the Content box.

3. Select a page size

4. Enter a caption

5. Enter an image resolution and select a colour model

6 Click here to select the layout format. This determines how many copies of the image are printed. Click OK in the Picture Package dialog box

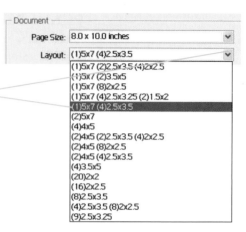

Document

Page Size: 8.0 x 10.0 inches

Layout: (1)5x7 (4)2.5x3.5

(1)5x7 (2)2.5x3.5 (4)2x2.5
(1)5x7 (2)3.5x5
(1)5x7 (8)2x2.5
(1)5x7 (4)2.5x3.25 (2)1.5x2
(1)5x7 (4)2.5x3.5
(2)5x7
(4)4x5
(2)4x5 (2)2.5x3.5 (4)2x2.5
(2)4x5 (8)2x2.5
(2)4x5 (4)2.5x3.5
(4)3.5x5
(20)2x2
(16)2x2.5
(8)2.5x3.5
(4)2.5x3.5 (8)2x2.5
(9)2.5x3.25

When buying a printer, choose one that has borderless printing. This means that it can print to the very edge of the page. This is particularly useful for items such as files produced as a Picture Package.

7 Each Picture Package is created as a separate file and can be printed as required:

The Picture Package function is a useful one for printing images in a combination of sizes, such as for family portraits.

Picture Package @ 66.7% (Picture 1, RGB)

Real-world digital examples

One of the great things about digital photography is that it is fun. With Elements, images can be manipulated in a variety of ways – to the point where you may never trust a photograph again. This chapter shows how to create some commonly used effects, such as adding and removing items from images, creating collages and creating the impression of speed.

Covers

Chapter Twelve

Repairing old photographs

Enhancing digital images is not confined to those that are captured with a digital camera. Old photographs can also enjoy the same digital editing techniques – all that is required is for them to be scanned so that they are in a digital format. This is ideal for old images that have become faded, torn or creased. Once they have been scanned they can then be repaired in Elements. To do this:

Click on the Connect to Camera or Scanner button on the Welcome Screen to access scanners.

1 Select File>Import from the Menu bar, or click on the Import button in the Shortcuts bar and select your scanner from the list

2 Ensure that the image is scanned at a minimum resolution of 150 pixels per inch (ppi). This will create an image that is large enough to be printed out at a high quality and at a reasonable size. If you want to print the image at a size larger than 7 inches by 5 inches, scan it at a minimum of 300 ppi

The higher the resolution at which an image is scanned, the larger the resultant file size.

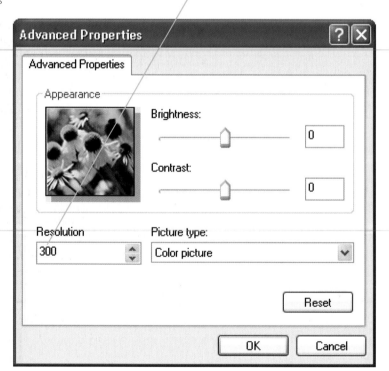

3   Select Enhance>Adjust Brightness/Contrast>Levels from the
    Menu bar

4   Drag the
    sliders to alter
    the black,
    white and
    midtone levels
    in the image.
    Click OK

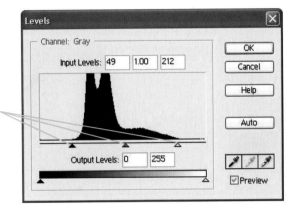

*Always make
digital copies of
old photographs
before you start
editing them.*

5   Select the Dodge
    tool from the
    Toolbox and
    drag it over any
    areas that need
    lightening

*See step 13 on
page 171 to
compare the
illustration on the
right with the
original unedited photograph.*

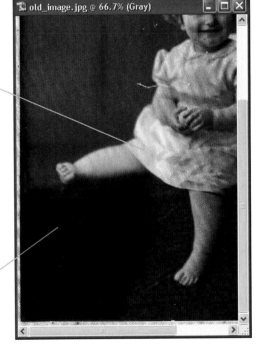

6   Select the Burn
    tool in the
    Toolbox and
    drag it over any
    areas that need
    darkening

7 Select the Zoom tool in the Toolbox and magnify any areas with creases or tears

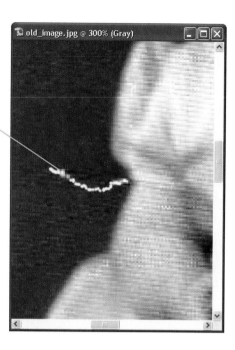

8 Select the Clone Stamp tool from the Toolbox:

9 Hold down Alt and click on the point that you want to use as the starting point for cloning

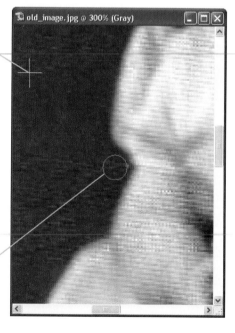

10 Drag the Cloning Stamp tool over the crease or tear

11 Apply colour correction techniques e.g. levels and contrast and brightness

12 The image after editing

13 Compare the result in step 12 with the image prior to editing

Removing unwanted items

On occasions you may want to remove certain items from an image, such as individual people from a group, or items such as buildings or objects that detract from the main subject in the image. If these items are at the edge of the image, they can be removed by cropping the image. However, if they are in the centre of the image they will have to be removed by cloning. It is then possible to rearrange a group so that it does not appear as if anyone, or anything, has been removed. To do this:

Do not select and delete parts of people that you want to keep in the final image.

1 Use the Polygonal Lasso tool to select the item to be removed. The selection does not have to be too accurate

2 Delete the selection from the image by selecting Edit> Clear from the Menu bar, or by pressing Delete (Windows) or Backspace (Mac) on the keyboard

3 Use the Polygonal Lasso tool to select the item to be moved. The selection does not have to be too accurate

The Clipboard is the area where items that have been cut or copied are stored, so that they can be pasted into the same, or another, file.

4 Select Edit>Cut from the Menu bar to remove the selection and place it on the Windows Clipboard

Selecting Edit>Cut from the Menu bar places an item on the Clipboard until another item is copied or cut. Selecting Edit>Clear removes the selected item permanently.

5 In the Layers palette, click here to add a new layer

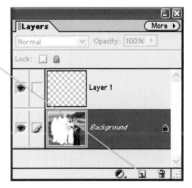

6 Select Edit>Paste from the Menu bar to place the selection on the new layer. Position it as required, using the Move tool:

7 Select the Eraser tool from the Toolbox and click and drag to remove any of the selection that is not required. You may want to magnify the selection with the Zoom tool:

8 Select the original layer and select the Clone Stamp tool:

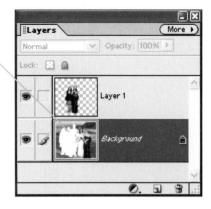

When working with multiple layers, lock any layers that are not being edited. This can be done by selecting them in the Layers palette and clicking on the Padlock icon. This will prevent you from editing them by mistake.

9 Hold down Alt and click to select the area to use to cover over the holes in the image. Change the cloning point frequently to create a smooth and accurate effect

If you want to get a better view when cloning the background layer, click the Eye icon next to the top layer so that the icon disappears. This will hide that layer's content, although it will still be in the image. Click the box where the Eye icon was to retrieve it and view the elements on that layer.

10 Fine-tune the image with any colour corrections e.g. brightness and contrast or levels

Adding people to a group

As well as removing people or objects from an image, there are also occasions when it is useful to add them to an image. This is particularly relevant for photographs of groups of people when someone was not available to appear in the original photograph. With a little help from Elements, it is possible to ensure that their absence was never even noticed. To do this:

If you can, when using an image of someone who you want to add to a group photograph, try to ensure that the lighting conditions are as similar as possible. This will save you some editing work when they are added to the group photograph.

Open the group photograph and select the group with the Polygonal Lasso tool. The selection does not have to be too accurate

2 Select Edit>Copy from the Menu bar to copy the selection of the group to the Clipboard

3 In the Layers palette, click here to add a new layer

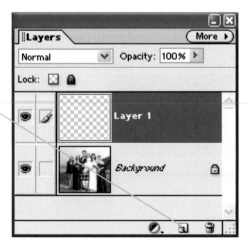

4 Select Edit>Paste from the Menu bar to place the selection on the new layer. Position it in exactly the same place as the background layer

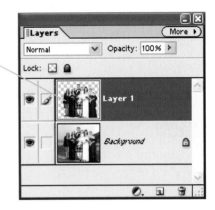

5 Select the Eraser tool from the Toolbox and click and drag to remove any of the selection that is not required. You may want to magnify the selection with the Zoom tool

6 Use the Polygonal Lasso tool to select the person who you want to add to the group image. Select Edit>Copy from the Menu bar

If required, select the Eraser tool in the Toolbox and drag to remove any unwanted areas around the selection of the individual being added.

7 Create a new layer, in between the two existing layers, and select Edit>Paste from the Menu bar to insert the selection of the individual

into the group image. This should be between the background layer and the top layer

To resize an image proportionally, hold down Shift and drag one of the corner resizing handles.

8 Select the middle layer then Image>Transform>Free Transform from the Menu bar. Drag the resizing handles to resize the individual in proportion with the rest of the image

If the original image appears to be inferior in quality to the individual you've added, try adding noise to the latter to make it more mottled.

9 Select the middle layer and apply colour corrections to match the tone, brightness and contrast of the other parts of the image

10 Select File>Save from the Menu bar and save the whole image as a Photoshop PSD file, to preserve the different layers so that they can be edited again, if required

Images with layers that are saved in the Photoshop PSD format are a lot larger in size than the same composite image (i.e. one that has had all of its layers flattened and is then saved in another format, such as JPEG).

11 Select Layer>Flatten Image from the Menu bar. This will amalgamate all of the layers

12 Select File>Save As from the Menu bar and save the flattened image in a format suitable for its intended use. The individual layers will not now be available in this format

Creating collages

Collages can be a very effective artistic use of digital images. This involves incorporating two or more images to give an unusual or surreal effect. There are a number of effects that can be created with collages but two of the main ones are:

Creating different sized objects

One of the striking effects that can be created with a collage is that of two elements that look incongruous, such as a very large person, dwarfing the background. To do this:

1   Work out the effect you want to achieve and capture two images accordingly:

When creating a collage from two images, try to capture both images under similar lighting conditions. This will remove the need to edit them too much once they have been combined.

2   Use the Polygonal Lasso tool to select the object that is going to be resized. Select Edit>Copy from the Menu bar

3 Select the background image and select Edit>Paste from the Menu bar to place the selection on a new layer

If a new layer is not already added, one will be inserted automatically when a selection is pasted into an existing image.

4 Select Image>Transform>Free Transform from the Menu bar and resize the selection as required

5 Make any colour corrections as required to make the two images match as closely as possible

Merging images

Another popular form of digital collage is when separate images are merged together through the use of layers. To do this:

1 Make a selection of an image or part of an image. Select Edit>Copy from the Menu bar

2 Open another image and select Edit>Paste from the Menu bar to add the selection, on a new layer

3 Drag the Layers palette
from the palette well.
Select a layer and click
here to select a
method for merging
the currently selected
layer with the one
below it

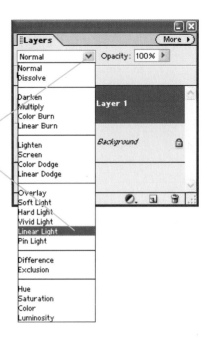

*The background
layer being at the
bottom of any
layered image, no
merge options are
available if it is selected.*

4 Add more selections as required and use different merge options
to create the final collage

Creating the impression of speed

When capturing images of moving vehicles or people it can be effective to create the impression of speed by making the background blurred while the main subject is static and in sharp focus. This can be done when taking the image itself (depending on the sophistication of the digital camera being used) or Elements can create the same effect. To do this:

1   Select the Polygonal or Magnetic Lasso tool from the Toolbox:

2   In the Options bar, set the Feather value to between 5–10 pixels:

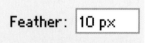

3   Make a selection as accurately as possible around the border of the vehicle or person

It is better to make the selection just inside the border of the object, rather than just outside it. This way, the border itself will be blurred and merge in with the background.

4   Select Edit>Cut from the Menu bar

5   Select Filter>Blur>Motion Blur from the Menu bar

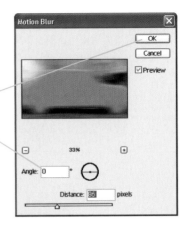

6 Select the required settings for the Motion Blur effect and click OK

7 The Motion Blur settings are applied to the whole of the remaining image

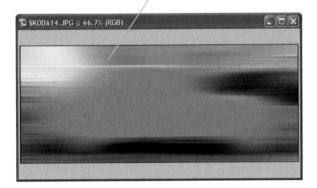

To further enhance the final image, select the wheels of the vehicle with the Elliptical Marquee tool and apply the same amount of Motion Blur as to the background. This will create the effect of the wheels spinning around.

8 Select Edit>Paste from the Menu bar to place the vehicle or person back in the image. The feathered edges should now merge with the blurred background

Simulating depth of field

Depth of field is a common photographic technique for changing the area of an image that is in focus. This is most frequently used to throw the background out of focus, thus giving the main subject greater emphasis. You can achieve the same effect in Elements:

1 Open an image and select the main subject using the Polygonal Lasso tool. Invert the selection by selecting Select>Inverse from the Menu bar

Simulating depth of field is effective for portraits in particular. By blurring the background, the main subject is given much greater emphasis.

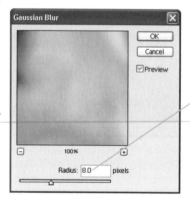

2 Select Filter>Blur>Gaussian Blur from the Menu bar and enter the required settings. Click OK

3 The blur effect is applied to the background, leaving the main subject in sharp focus

Index

I

J

L

M